I've enjoyed knowing Fred and his delightful wife, Gloria, since 1978. That's when he became a trustee of Baylor University Medical Center in Dallas.

Fred was recognized then, as now, as a gifted speaker. I've seen audiences react to his intense enthusiasm for the subject, no matter what the topic: leadership, the Christian experience, and life itself. He has a wide breadth of experience from which to draw. This very readable book reveals Fred's great insight as he attempts to impart some of the lessons life has taught him.

You'll find reading this book is an enjoyable experience.

Boone Powell Jr.

LET'S TALK

Ideas To Trigger Family Conversation

Fred Roach

THE
DONNING COMPANY
PUBLISHERS

Library of Congress Cataloging in Publication Data

Roach, Fred.
   Let's talk.

   Includes index.
   1.   Meditations.   2.   Christian life—1960–
I.   Title.
BV4832.2.R55   248'.4   77-13347
ISBN 0-8007-0908-X

To my wife, Gloria, who is a constant source of strength in living the full and abundant life;

My daughter, Valerie, who is an inspiration and joy to me through the beauty I see in her;

My son, Bob, to whom, because of my deep love for him, I enjoy saying, "Let's talk";

My mother, Kathleen, for her strength in being both a mother and father to me and for raising me to appreciate God's plan for my life;

My secretary, Barbara Vick, for her steadfastness and gracious spirit;

And the many people who have influenced what I have said in this book.

A Note to the Reader

I love the idea of *sharing*—the dynamic that happens when we're involved in the building of relationships. The ideas in this book were written for one major purpose—to build a stronger relationship between my son, Bob, and myself. And it did!

Looking back sixteen years to when I wrote these notes, I did not know the impact they might have on Bob's life, Gloria's, and my life, as well as many others. I am grateful for the testimony of many who have said my notes have positively affected their lives.

As you read my personal notes to our son, notes that were never intended to be published, please recognize that they reflect my personal background and were not meant to be a theoretical treatise about life, or even a theological challenge, but rather practical thoughts that a father felt might positively affect his son, as well as our entire family.

As I wrote one note each day for a year, our entire family was drawn closer together as we used these ideas to create a fun time of family discussion. With Bob at 15 and Valerie at 17, this generated a fantastic synergistic effect within our family.

The sequel of events finds Bob involved in a very successful real estate and homebuilding career. Our daughter, Valerie, is now the mother of six wonderful boys, who give us, as grandparents, great . . .

Joy On the Journey,

Fred Roach
1992

Contents

Aspirations   15

While the slope may sometimes be sharp and steep, both the thrill of the climb and the exhilaration of reaching the top are worth the effort.

Accountability   49

God's stewardship requires that we give ourselves completely—everything that we have and everything that we are.

Faith   69

You have no assurance from the indifferent; you sense an assurance from your friends; you are satisfied of the assurance from those who love you, but you can have absolute assurance in your perfect Maker and Saviour—Jesus Christ.

Relationships   83

One of the most real evidences of Christ's presence in our lives is whether we reach out and touch the lives of those around us.

Maturing   111

What one person sees as failure is merely a stepping-stone for us.

Gifts   157

God's Word teaches that from those to whom much is given, much is required.

Preface

Dear Bobby,

In days ahead I'm going to try to write you a note on different subjects that you can consider, and then we can visit together and discuss them.

I believe you know how much I love you and how I want you to have the best in all the world. There's nothing that I wouldn't do to give you the means for a happy, successful life. I believe I can do this best by helping you reach your personal potential.

I also realize that I affect your future more by what I am and do than by what I say. So, as I write to you I am reminding myself of the same effective standards of life.

In Proverbs 4:1, Solomon wrote, "Hear, ye children, the instruction of a father . . . ." I know that many people have had a tremendous impact in my life, including many father figures, since my father died when I was just a young boy. What I have to say will be influenced by this background. But, more important, I will be seeking God's leadership in what I share with you.

Study the information that we'll be reviewing. Let it sink in and affect your life. Reread it from time to time and see if you can tell if you sense a more positive view toward life. Life should have a vitality, an excitement! Don't let anything rob you of this.

Jesus said toward the end of the Sermon on the Mount: "Therefore, whosoever *heareth* these sayings of mine, and *doeth* them, I will liken him unto a wise man, which built his house upon a rock." The words I write won't be as profound as those of Christ, but if you live by them, your life will be full and exciting. Learn to live by God's command: "Give yourself completely to God—every part of you."

Written because of my deep love for you,

Dad.

Foreword

Breakfast conversation that morning at Dallas Country Club was in full swing, animated as usual. It was the first Friday of the month—a time of regular fellowship among fifteen Dallas Christian business executives which has become a cherished and treasured tradition in the life of each. It is simply an informal monthly get-together during which fifteen men who head their businesses compare experiences and share exciting reports of what the Lord Jesus Christ is doing to them, through them, for them, and all too often, in spite of them.

Fred Smith and Clark Breeding were on my left talking across me to Ford Madison and Don Kerr on my right. At the other end of the table, Lee Slaughter was the center of a conversational group including Tommy Jones, Cullum Thompson, Fred Roach, and Bill McKenzie. Lawson Ridgeway, Don Test, and Ed Yates were into a subject of their own. Bill Seay and Bill Mead, completing our group, were out of town.

Those at my end of the table were lamenting today's sad decrease in writing skills and in written communication between people, especially family and loved ones, because of television and the telephone. As an outstanding example of the old-fashioned lost art of letter writing, Fred Smith was telling our group about a fascinating, rare out-of-print book he was reading entitled *The Upton Letters*. Written in 1904 by an anonymous schoolteacher in Upton, England, they were simply his attempts to encourage, comfort, and entertain a dying friend. Sender and recipient remain forever anonymous, identified only by initials. Although never meant for publication, they were published by the friend's widow in accordance with his deathbed request.

As Fred described the book in conversational tones too low to be heard across the room, he was suddenly interrupted by Lee Slaughter at the other end of the table.

"I'd like to tell you fellows a little story," said Lee, raising his voice loud enough to be heard by everyone. For the first time that morning, one man commanded the attention of the entire group.

"As some of you know," said Lee, "it is traditional in my company at Christmas to gather for a company-wide assembly to which we usually invite an outstanding speaker. Last December we had the pleasure of listening to Fred Roach. It is difficult for me to describe the impact of his testimony upon the lives of some of our employees. For example, just last week at a convention in New Orleans, one of my employees reminded me of Fred's remarks. It seems Fred has written a personal longhand letter to his fifteen-year-old son, Bobby, every day for an entire year, outlining his philosophy of life, his spiritual beliefs, his faith in the private-enterprise system—anything that came into his mind."

I listened to Lee in complete amazement at this conversational coincidence. Loving your son is one thing. Loving him enough to be willing to pour out your basic thoughts and beliefs in writing every day for a whole year is something else. Here in our very group was the modern counterpart of *The Upton Letters*. The Lord's timing was too obvious to ignore.

When Lee had finished, I took the floor, telling the rest about Fred Smith's discussion up at my end of the table.

"Gentlemen, it seems to me that the unbelievable timing of these two conversations simply cannot be ignored. I realize Fred Roach's letters are the private property of his son, Bobby, and were not written for the public. Just the same, if Bobby doesn't object, I think Fred should have them published. If he does, I think one of us should do the preface for the book. His readers will be interested in knowing how they came to be published."

After a little gentle prodding from the rest of us, Fred Roach agreed to send the letters to a publisher.

The editors saw a broader use for family communication. The material would be excellent for sparking serious and inspired conversation when family members shared time together.

The result, *Let's Talk,* is the volume you hold in your hands. You will find it to contain the distillation of the wisdom, experience, love, and faith of a man who has been preeminently successful in the business world and who has been wise enough to give credit where credit belongs—to the Lord Himself. This should be required reading for every Christian father and family member.

DONALD F. MITCHELL

Aspirations

While the slope may sometimes be sharp and steep, both the thrill of the climb and the exhilaration of reaching the top are worth the effort.

Today

On my specially printed "To Do" list are these words: "Today is the first day of the rest of my life," and this verse from Proverbs 16:3: "Commit your work to the Lord, then it will succeed" (LB).

Today is a great day. It can become all I make of it. I can fashion for myself a day that includes new experiences; a day in which I push myself to new limits; a day that can become exciting as I relate to people and share with them. Today really can be a great day.

The problem with most of us is we wait for tomorrow to tackle those tough jobs, to begin our diets, to get to those lists of things that need to be done. Acting today forces us to get all systems up and working. Then today will be better, and tomorrow will also be better.

Now! Today! There's no better time to resolve to meet our goals; no better time to get on with getting the job done; no better time to enjoy the fruits of our efforts. The rewards of recognizing the potential of today are fantastic. Enjoy them!

Intentions

There's little value to good intentions, unless we follow through on them. Over and over again I find in myself the frustration of unfulfilled intentions. And there's little reason for this futility since most things we intend to do require very little time or effort.

It's true that I'm overoptimistic about my ability to get a job done; so I say yes many times when I ought to give more consideration to the matter. My intentions are good, but perhaps even impossible to execute. In fact, I'm sure it would be better if I would limit my acceptance of tasks to those I really intend to complete on a timely basis.

The processes of the mind determine those deep, personal intentions. These determine our ultimate direction. Sometimes our intentions are good and at other times negative—on purpose. Some even try to stay in neutral—with the desire to have no intentions.

It would seem that our goal should be to be realistic in definitely setting our intentions. If reasonable, and positive in nature, while at the same time challenging, it will help us mature.

Planning

Our lives need order and direction. Developing planning capability within us will provide this great asset. Lack of plans brings chaos to any area you approach—business, family, or meeting social needs.

Begin early in life to establish plans. Plan—then execute. Even fail. It's a process that provides maturity. No one ever arrived unless he began.

You can tell a lot about a person, a church, a family, or a business by how they plan. It makes sense to plan the most effective use of our time and resources. Good planning is important.

Learn how to plan. Always plan for success. Never give up! Discipline yourself! Change plans when it seems appropriate! Good planning can multiply your effort. The fun of seeing accomplished things for which you've planned will be rewarding.

Programmed

Some people are programmed to the point of perpetual performance. While we live in a fairly rigid, culturally programmed society, we still need to maintain our personal God-centered direction.

Everyone wants to give input into the programming process. Obviously, I want to help shape the direction of your life. I believe this is a part of the proper stewardship of my life. This is not possession but rather direction. Others want their input too: your teachers, your peers, your government—in fact, all of society.

A properly designed program helps us in being progressive. We feed into our programs the "givens" in life such as "I want to do well in school"; "I don't have any desire to harm my life with drugs." If we build into life's program these absolutes, we can then get on with the real fun part of the programming effort.

The nature of our goals in life determines the detail of the programming process. A good programmer builds on what's in his memory bank. The best programmer maintains a high degree of flexibility—a real freedom to keep growing.

Goals

I said at the beginning of the year that I wanted each month of this year to be complete in itself—in which I could acknowledge some progress. I set goals and with God's help reached most of them—although not all. They'll be added to next month's list again.

In my business my goals were very specific. They related to property, product, people, and profit. We met just about every one of these goals. For example, we beat our profit projection by over two hundred thousand dollars, and we made good progress on property acquisition.

I met a goal to get together a group of men as prayer partners. I failed in meeting a goal to see all the men in my Sunday-school class. I also failed in sharing with someone on a one-to-one basis about Christ and seeing them accept Jesus Christ as Saviour— although when I shared publicly, several made first-time decisions for Christ or renewed commitments to Christ.

I believe in goals, but I'm not frustrated when I fail to meet one—just more determined to try again with God's help. Remember—set goals, all kinds. They will help you determine progress, and success will give a real sense of accomplishment.

Vision

Our pastor, Dr. Earl Craig, today shared something about his long-term vision for our church. It is exciting! It is exciting to anticipate how God wants us to accomplish His will in the future. Then, this afternoon the long-range planning committee met to begin to sense God's direction for our church in the future.

I'm also excited about the vision of Dr. James Landes, executive director of our Texas Baptist General Convention, for how Texas Baptists can share the gospel message with the millions of unchurched in Texas. He is beginning to implement a four-year plan that I'm sure will be revolutionary. It involves mobilizing Christians for the task of evangelism. I'm glad to be a part of this planning effort.

Men, and nations, without a vision, perish. I'm thankful for your ability to focus in on the future. It's great to see you anticipating your life goals which include possibly becoming a medical doctor and then retiring early and teaching. Maintain a vision! Ask God to focus it for you! Move out to accomplish it! Everything you are doing has an effect on your ultimate success in achieving your goals.

Journey

You've heard me dozens of times talk about the concept of *journey*. It's a good word. It's active, moving, exciting, factual! In our lay-renewal work we speak of "Journey Into Life-style Evangelism." We talk about being on a spiritual journey, or spiritual pilgrimage.

Today Dr. Craig's sermon topic was "How Do I Know When I've Arrived" from Joshua 1:6–11. He shared from the book *Journey Into Usefulness* by James Mahoney. It was an exciting sermon about how many times we get to the edge of the Promised Land and fail to move, or journey, in.

There's fullness of life available to each of us, and we *can* find it. Just as on any trip we take, we use a road map, the same is true of the journey of life. The best road map is God's Word—the Bible.

Our journey is full of joy and peace. At times there are crises, at other times, change in direction. We meet exciting people on the journey. It's fun! My journey is unique, as is yours. For a while we share a common direction, but then we're on our own. *Always* we're led along by God Himself.

Fullness

Never be satisfied with less than fullness. I like the little booklet *How to Have a Full and Meaningful Life,* distributed by the Sunday School Board of our Southern Baptist Convention. It describes how a person can come into proper relation with God through Jesus Christ.

God intends that we have a full life; yet most of us are forever seeking rather than claiming the fullness that is ours. Fullness as a concept is the same for all of us—to be complete, whole. It embodies different characteristics because of our uniqueness in God's purpose, but it isn't some secret that God is keeping from us.

It's enjoying the here and now. It's releasing ourselves completely to God every day. It's being a well-rounded person now, not just looking forward to what will happen next year or five years from now.

While you'll be growing physically, mentally, emotionally, and spiritually in future years, you can have a fullness, wholeness, now and each day of your life. Never look only to the future for fullness. Enjoy it now.

Formula

Everyone has his formula for success—in selling, in raising a family, in church, and in every other aspect of life. These various formulas can be very helpful in keeping our lives well regulated. They can, in effect, help us in our self-discipline. But we must be careful that we don't get to the point that we think everything can be set down in a simple one, two, three.

The book *Lord, Make My Life a Miracle* by Raymond Ortlund has a simple but profound formula for the full and abundant life: (1) establish a right relationship to God through His Son, Jesus Christ, and let God's Holy Spirit direct your life; (2) then establish a solid relationship within the Body of Christ, the church; (3) then reach out to the world to share the beauty of the Good News of Christ. It is a formula simple to understand but hard to implement. I pray that both of us can put this one into effect in our lives.

Victories

One of the keys to success is to recognize when you have succeeded. We need to mentally attune ourselves to the fact of victory in our pursuits. This past week I challenged three prayer partners to list a victory each day. This morning one of the men was tremendously excited as he shared the victories of the past week. It was a week when he had more sales than in any single week before, and he shared a real victory with his son who surrendered his life for full-time Christian service.

We need to be very sensitive to the good things that happen in our lives. It's good mental discipline to find the best thing that happens each day and to thank God for it. On my list this past week was the fun of being with you at our church's Royal Ambassador camp for boys and your sister Valerie's having been named a Merit Scholar.

Victories tend to multiply when we become more aware of them. They become stepping-stones to a victorious life. Pray for specific help from God and then celebrate the victories.

Revival

Our church is in the middle of its fall revival. Generally we Christians fail to take advantage of these types of services as a renewing of our personal lives. I believe it's essential to step back periodically and take a look at what's happening, both in us and around us.

I remember your decision for Christ was made at a revival service where Rev. Neal Jones, a guest evangelist from Washington, D.C., was our preacher. Since that time you have had tremendous opportunity to grow closer to God. You've heard and shared with some of the best evangelists in the world.

Use this time of revival to recommit yourself to Christ. Consciously seek a closer relationship with God. Determine that you will develop an intimacy with God that goes beyond that first-time experience.

I seek for myself, our family, our church, and our community a fresh, new experience with Christ.

Freshness

One of my favorite verses is Romans 12:2 in the Living Bible where it says we're to have a "fresh newness" about us. I like that word *fresh*. It has a clean, crisp sound.

I like to see people who have that fresh look in all they do.
I like to see people tackle problems with an open, fresh approach.
I like to see directions set and priorities established with a fresh look.
I like to see God's freshness show through the lives of His followers.

I love to brainstorm ideas. Usually we come up with innovations when we don't hem ourselves in mentally. Recently I worked on an incentive program for our salespeople. Fresh ideas popped into my mind as I let down all human barriers.

You can afford to be new, different—fresh. Don't let people or situations bottle you up. Stay fresh and innovative. This is what most people want to see and what creates real worth in people.

Transformed

We do not have to stay the same. We can grow into better people. The Bible says: "Be not conformed to this world: but be ye transformed by the renewing of your mind . . . (Romans 12:2). This teaches, and I have experienced, that transformation of our lives or actions is accomplished on a mental basis. Spiritually speaking, God's power at work within us is transforming us to the point of being mentally renewed.

I like the books by Tim LaHaye including *Spirit-Controlled Temperament* and *Transformed Temperaments.* They tell us how this transformation can take place. Simplified, it's our willingness to let God work in our lives to build up our strengths and to help us overcome our weaknesses.

Always remember that with God's help you can change. While I see little in your life that needs serious change, you can attack those small things of which you're aware better than anyone else. You'll discover the joy of seeing life from a new perspective through God's transformation.

Change

One thing of which we can be certain is change. I'm changing. You're changing. Our family structure and relationships are changing. Accept change as being natural. It opens new doors of discovery.

Seek the maximum good from change. Learn from it. To reminisce is natural, but it should never keep us from life's forward direction. Change is expansive. We see new things, meet new people, make new friends—all accomplished without losing old friends or the past.

Those who refuse to change—die—either physically, mentally, emotionally, or spiritually. Change, then, should be a growing, maturing aspect of life. Take advantage of change. Use it to better yourself.

Reconciliation

To be in balance is a good feeling. *Reconciliation* is a word that indicates that things are in balance, or the word can be used in a financial, political, social, or even spiritual sense.

To be in harmony with God and the world requires the reconciliation accomplished in the life of Jesus Christ. He said He reconciled the world to Himself. He also said we are to be the means of reconciliation.

Try hard to stay in balance with everything around you. Obviously, this starts within yourself. Keep things together mentally, so there's minimum internal conflict. Seek the peace of God. Also stay in harmony with your family. Then keep reconciled with current activities and life's goals.

It's a good feeling to be in harmony with your surroundings. Try hard to accomplish this.

Unity

"United we stand; divided we fall." The importance of unity has always been understood by man. With our mental eye we can see:

the beauty of a family bound together,
the beauty of a nation dedicated to a unity of purpose,

the beauty of the church united to share the Good News
of Jesus Christ,

the beauty of a community committed to solve man's
common needs.

One of the problems in our society today is fragmentation. In the midst of people, there is the danger of being isolated. Unity requires effort—whether in a marriage, a family, or any other organization. Since this is true, we need to commit ourselves to be unifying in our personal effort.

This unity, or harmony, should be sought in all life's relationships. It will provide a solid platform upon which to grow. The pluses that will be added to your life will be immeasurable.

You Can

The Calvary Baptist Church of Columbia, Missouri, wrapped up their second lay-renewal weekend today. I shared at the morning worship service on the subject "You Can." There's nothing that God wants the church or any individual in the church to do that they can't accomplish using the power available through God Himself.

I referred to the "can-do" stores around the country—hardware stores that sell items so we can fix it ourselves. While I might buy items in these stores for Mom rather than myself, the idea is that we *can do* a lot when we want to. The problem with most of us is that we begin with the wrong premise—"I can't."

Man's ingenuity seems virtually unlimited. We have accomplished more in the last half century from the standpoint of man's knowledge than in all the preceding span of man's existence. Man has pushed himself to fantastic limits by saying, "I can." We must remember that "we can" because of God-given attributes and not let ourselves become excessively ego centered. Yes, "you can" and "I can" with our God-given abilities and uniqueness when we put our trust in Him.

Doing

Doing means activity. The aim of the Miami Baptist Association this year is *doing* what it senses God wants done. I pay men for *doing* their jobs, not for *wanting* to get their jobs done. You get good grades for learning—not because you simply have the desire to learn. You will become a leader in any particular group when they see you are a "doer." The Scripture verse that children sing highlights this truth: "Be ye doers of the word, and not hearers only . . ." (James 1:22).

I'm a Christian brother, not when I *say* I'm a brother, but when I *do* what a brother does—love, share, hurt. *Being* builds relationships, not just thinking, wanting, or saying.

Doing also builds confidence. It helps us learn our capabilities. Fear to *do* robs us of life's richest blessings. On the other hand, *doing* provides us with life's golden moments.

Resolve

Personal resolve sets parameters in our lives that help give direction. The lack of resolve leads to fear and indecision.

We sometimes resolve together and sometimes on a personal basis. A lawyer would say, "I hereby resolve," or "We do hereby resolve." It makes definitive our intention to accomplish a specific act or to follow a certain direction. But whether we formalize our decisions into legal documents, or not, we still need to make resolutions—and not only on New Year's Day each year.

Resolutions affect every area of our lives. As we mature and as we sense a progressive revelation about life, we should strive for a concept of progressive resolution.

Resolve to do positive things—then grow. Never resolve to keep doing things that detract from your life or the lives of others. The day-by-day resolutions you make will affect the degree of happiness in your life.

Growth

The grass is growing; you're growing; our church is growing; Dallas is growing. Growth is beautiful. I especially like to see our investment account in the growth posture—as you have it now.

How you feel about the need to grow will impact what you accomplish in life. Some growth, maturing, is natural. I see this in you, physically. Other forms of growth are fairly automatic such as the level of intelligence. You will learn—that's a fact! But the degree to which you learn is a matter of self-determination. If you make up your mind, your intellect can grow to fantastic levels.

Other forms of growth are not at all automatic. You don't grow spiritually by accident or on an automatic basis. You grow spiritually, because you decide to. It's a commitment to growth that puts us in a position of reaching toward spiritual maturity.

Growth is good! Seek it in all areas of your life. While growing, keep all areas in balance. Grow socially, intellectually, physically, and spiritually.

Security

Everyone is looking for security of one kind or another. Some are looking for financial security; others, for a way to secure for themselves good health; still others are concerned for ultimate security throughout eternity. Even those who throw off the restraints of our society are looking for an elusive security that they feel will come from being free to do as they please.

To want to be secure is natural. It's one of the chief motivations for success in business and many industries, including the life-insurance industry. It's a key force in the home-building industry, which is the second largest industry in our country.

While the desire for security is universal, we must be careful that it doesn't become an obsession with us—that it's not the key motivator in all our decisions. The desire for security—financial or other forms—cannot replace our need for faith and trust in God as related to our futures. We obviously must be prudent, but we must never replace our ingenuity for the perfect security we find in God.

Plateaus

Man seems to crave the plateaus of life. We reach one plateau and then see the potential of that next plateau. This is good. The danger comes when we get to where we're not willing to strive for that next plateau. I see thousands of people on various plateaus unwilling to take the risk to move to a higher one.

While the slopes may sometimes be sharp and steep, both the thrill of the climb and the exhilaration of reaching the top are worth all the effort. Imagine the picture of those unwilling to try, holding back and missing the excitement that comes with success.

I see these plateaus in every area of our lives: in the business world, in our spiritual lives, in our family lives—in all things. It doesn't make sense to strike out to reach that next plateau in business and fail to move forward in our relationship with God. The thrust forward needs to be for the *total man*—not in just part of our lives.

So, look ahead! See where that next plateau is and move toward achieving it. Have fun in the process. It's as enjoyable as the achievement.

Stand

I like Watchman Nee's book *Sit, Walk, Stand*. It would be good for you to study this book and see how we're to stand as followers of Christ.

How do we stand? In our own strength? Or in place of

another? We even use the term *stand-in*. Who is our stand-in before God? We know that answer: Jesus, our Saviour!

We are also told: ". . . God is able to make him stand" (Romans 14:4). Try this. Stand up—very tall and straight. Take a deep breath. Now exhale. Doesn't this make you feel good as the oxygen flows to your brain and you exhale the stale air from within you? While we're doing this physical exercise, we can do the same spiritually. We can stand tall, breathe in God's infilling Spirit, and exhale the sin and impurities in our lives.

I wish I could stand taller physically; yet it's hard with my back. But spiritually there's no limitation. I can mentally prepare myself to accept Christ's cleansing and to enjoy the blessings of standing for and with Jesus Christ.

Respect

Respect is something we should both seek and give. We seek respect by how we live. We gain respect by our actions. We lose the respect of others when there's a lack of dependability. We compromise respect when we rationalize every situation.

Just as we need to earn the respect of others, we also need to learn to give respect. Respect of others does not always mean agreement. I can respect another person and not necessarily agree with his views. We should have the right to disagree and to maintain relationships.

Respect for others is hard when you are violent in your disagreement. Yet aggressive confrontation accomplishes little. If we are to win people over to positive Christlikeness, it cannot be done with undue pressure. Respect requires love—a quality difficult to maintain when there's disagreement.

You will have the respect of others as you give respect to others. Do all in your strength to garner for yourself man's respect, but remember—ultimately your goal is to please God, not man.

Missionary

Very early in my life, I became aware of missionaries. I had two aunts who were missionaries—one to China and the other to the Mexican people. There was a special aura about them— something different.

Today's missionaries don't want to be different. Of course they're different from the world but not from other Christians who have turned over their lives to Christ. They are called to their mission field just as God set me aside to work in the business world.

We sometimes think it "costs" them more; yet God asks each of us to give ourselves completely to Him—every part of us. It's true that they suffer from being away from home and many times from loved ones and friends. And their living conditions aren't the best, as you and I experienced with Dr. Dan Gruver, the only medical missionary to the twenty-five thousand Cuna Indians in the San Blas Islands off Panama. Yet I've never met a happier, more fulfilled person.

In a sense we're all missionaries, followers of Christ, sent out on missions. I think maybe we all ought to be "set aside" and "sent out."

Victory in Jesus

When I was your age, two of my favorite songs were "Victory in Jesus" and "On to Victory." I wanted victory. I longed for it. I sought it and found it. The only real sense of victory I've ever had has come through my relationship with Jesus.

Sometimes when I'm away from you, I have this fantastic desire to have you with me to share experiences with me, to love me, and to let me demonstrate my love for you. I visualize you and sense the warmth of my memory of you; yet you're not there, and I hurt.

I have the same kind of desire for an intimate relationship with Jesus. I also love Him and want Him to love me. I visualize Him and sense the warmth of my memory of great times together. But here's the difference—He's here with me, in me, around me. I can have an intimate relationship with Him in prayer and sharing. I can have immediate "Victory in Jesus." Realize the magnitude of this tremendous resource we have as Christians, as children of the King, to whom victory is assured.

Quote

I try to remember good quotes. We come across some interesting people as we move around, and they have a lot to say to us. If sound, then we'll want to remember what's said; so we can share it with others. In fact, as we then share it with others, it becomes more important to us.

I like to use a book of quotations. There are some "gems" there that can convey ideas very succinctly. When I use this type of quote, I always try to give credit to the person quoted. We don't want to claim ideas or words for ourselves if they belong to others. At the same time, a quote can trigger a thought process within us that is unique to us. God can influence us mentally, so we can gain key spiritual insights. We have the responsibility to pass that insight on to others.

Learn from others. Pass it on to others. Be an intellectual conduit that will create a strong chain that binds people together over the span of time and distance.

Philosophy

Yesterday I read Valerie's philosophy of life. She had written it for her English literature class. It was entitled "Joy—the Magic Formula." It was profound, particularly for a seventeen-year-old. It zeroed in on the keys to joy in our lives—Jesus, others, and ourselves. She then pinpointed how we should relate to each.

All of us develop a philosophy of life. Most of us don't take time to write it out in an essay, even though it would be a good discipline to do so. We don't even codify it in our minds, but the fact still remains that we have, or are continuing to develop, a personal philosophy that affects what we do and what we are.

I believe the happiest people are those that understand themselves and their environment. We thus gain an insight into the "whys" of life. I sense that you are a person who has a pretty clear picture of your philosophy of life. It's important that we let God focus for us the needed changes in our personal philosophies. In the end, we still want to let God mold and shape our lives.

Counseling

You went off tonight to learn how to be a good camp counselor. Being a counselor means that you will be involved in counseling younger boys. I believe you will do a good job, because you have it "all together." The possibility of Valerie's becoming a Christian psychologist is also exciting, and she, too, is well equipped for that kind of profession.

Giving advice or counsel to another person should be approached very carefully. A friend of mine wanted you to counsel him on an investment in the stock market, but I discouraged it, because even though you've studied it, you would probably make almost as many poor selections as good ones. Of course, time will correct this for you.

I've had some rewarding experiences from trying to help others. My approach is more as a friendly listener and prayer partner than as any expert in counseling. Other lay people I know have tried to be professional and got in over their heads and hurt themselves and others.

In your camp activity, be sensitive to the way the young men look up to you. Be a good leader. Give good, solid counsel. The best counsel you can give is to live for Jesus and point others to Him.

Speaking

Tonight I speak at a teacher-appreciation dinner. I look forward to it, and I feel that God led me to accept this opportunity. Next week I will share at a men's meeting at another church.

I sense a real responsibility as I approach these meetings. People are taking their very precious time to try to be more effective in their Christian lives; so I must ask God to lead me as I challenge them and attempt to motivate them to a deeper walk with Christ.

The key for you to remember as you get to the point where you speak to groups—either at school or church—is the message you want to convey. This requires that you understand your audience and what will move them to action. It also requires that you set down your thoughts in a logical, sequential manner. I've found it best to speak to groups just like I'd talk to one of them about the same subject. It's fun to share ideas and concepts with groups. Learn this yourself through experience.

Wisdom

We've said before that wisdom is more than knowledge, and knowledge is more than miscellaneous stored data. Wisdom indicates a sense of being wise. How does this happen? Obviously, I can't make you wise. I can't give you wisdom.

Wisdom requires an unusual ability to absorb what we're taught, what we observe, in order to put into proper relationship all the influences in our lives. There's a sorting process—an intellectual digesting—to arrive at the right answer.

Recently, I've been studying the Book of Proverbs. The first nine chapters deal with the writer's exhortation to his son about wisdom. I guess the letters this past year were for the same purpose—to exhort you to respond to the proper influences in your life.

Wisdom comes first by trusting God and giving reverence to Him. As Rev. Gordon Highfill, our assistant pastor, said last Sunday, we need to *really* worship God, to acknowledge how much we love Him.

Never mistake the characteristics of real wisdom. Wisdom is like love—never haughty. The wise person has a humble spirit and is not overly proud. Seek this wisdom in your life. With it you'll avoid mediocrity.

Knowledge

Knowledge, historically, has grown at an arithmetic rate. While in the twentieth century, we've seen it grow geometrically. There is available a storehouse of knowledge that baffles our imaginations. We have developed into a highly specialized society.

I believe knowledge is fine to seek but only to achieve our ultimate goals in life. While I'm technically trained as an accountant, I consider myself a generalist. I hope I have learned to relate to more than the financial side of life.

Knowledge is more than information. Accumulating data moves toward knowledge when we get to the point we know how to use the information to accomplish something. Knowledge assumes a useful purpose, even if that purpose is simply personal mental pleasure.

To know indicates an intimacy. This is how we are to relate to God. We are to know Him through the revelation of Jesus Christ. Don't depend on information about God, but develop that vital, intensive personal relationship that brings knowledge and joy.

Hope

As an optimist, I have a lot of hope, a confidence in the future.

I have a hope in what I'm in the process of becoming.
I have a hope in what I see you becoming.
I have a hope that our nation will continue to become.
I have a basic hope in God's directing all of us to
become what we can be.

Hope is not empty speculation. The combination of hope and faith moves toward an absolute trust, a certainty as to the ultimate outcome. I have a real hope and trust in you. I also see that hope being fleshed out in what I see you becoming. Your determination and maturity are very evident. This same hope which you have—encourage in others. A common vision for the future—and hope and trust to see it fulfilled—is a beautiful thing to see unfold.

Future

It's been said that we don't know what the future holds for us, but we know who holds the future. I have no blueprint of what my life is going to be like tomorrow or any time in the future, yet I know that God has a blueprint of my life—a perfect plan for me. My task is not to know the future but rather to have absolute faith and hope to the point that I'm doing what I sense God wants me to do now.

While I don't know the future, I know my present is largely the result of decisions I've made in the past. It follows then, that the future will be governed by decisions that I make today. Therefore, if I want to control my future to the maximum extent possible, I'll take the necessary action now.

I know my future will be full of love, joy, and peace, because I decide each day to release myself totally to the direction of God. I know my body will be as healthy as possible, because I made the decision when I was a teenager that I would never defile my body—the temple of Christ—with alcohol, drugs, and cigarettes. While I can't fully control the future, I can assure myself of an exciting walk with Christ.

Relevant

Maintain relevancy in your life. So much time, talk, and energy is wasted by people on things that aren't in the least bit relevant. Obviously, relevancy is not absolute. What's relevant to me might not be for you. This requires an understanding nature on our part as we become involved in the interplay between people.

Sometimes it can be difficult to decide what's relevant. That's no problem. Don't worry about it; just move on. Strive to make your total life count. There will be some wasted motion, but overall you'll enjoy a fulfilling experience.

Relevant growth requires sequential effort. You're building a structure, so you want to make sure that the foundation is well set—broad enough and strong enough to build a life upon. Then as the building stones are stacked upon each other, they begin to form a beautiful structure that becomes your life. It's a great, enjoyable process—living out the relevant life.

Purpose

This is one of my favorite words—*purpose*. In all things, there is purpose. God purposed to create man. He purposed to give man a free will. His purpose was for man to enjoy all of life.

To see God's purpose, gives our lives purpose. When I know I'm in God's purpose—and I am usually very aware of this—

then I have real peace and joy in my life. On the other hand, when my sin separates me temporarily from God's perfect will for me, then I have a sense of confusion and lack of direction.

There are a number of forces in our lives that set our purposes. Our basic culture helps shape our purposes as do the social forces at work in the community. Our personal economic positions—our concepts of the importance of money—also help establish our personal goals and purposes.

Don't just do things by accident or by rote. Use all available resources to incorporate purpose into who you are, what you do, and what you stand for.

Quality

One of the things about which we have to be careful is quality. The company for which I worked before had a "Seal of Quality." It stood for something. There was no compromise when it came to delivery of quality—whatever the cost.

Quality applies to so much of life—in fact, to life itself. We ought to seek quality and utility in all that we do and in everything we provide others.

Someone has said, "If the job is worth doing, it's worth doing right." We ought to think quality in everything we do: in our jobs, in building relations with people, in personal habits. The casual approach—where nothing really matters—can't be a very satisfying kind of life.

Quality can become a basic concept in everything we do—if we work at it. I believe it's the soundest approach to life and will bring its own rewards. Stamp into your life this "Seal of Quality."

Integrity

Integrity is not something you say; it's what you are. It has many connotations depending on each individual's personal bias and training. While truth is absolute, integrity is harder to categorize in absolute terms. My view of attitudes that demonstrate integrity are different from those of some of my associates.

Integrity implies truth, trust, honesty, fairness—and more. I sense that real integrity is more than ethical, moral, social, or economic integrity. I believe, rather, it relates to the total man. To me, the word *integrity* relates to the word *integral*—all the parts making up the whole.

From a business standpoint, I want our company to be known as a company with integrity, which simply means the people in the company have integrity. Personally, this is a goal that I have—to be trustworthy, honest, fair, ethical, moral, and all the other things that demonstrate real integrity. Strive for this in your life. It's a key to a happy life.

Whole

I love the concept of being whole—complete. While many forces from within and from without pull us in many directions, life is intended to be lived in harmony.

While I strive to be a whole person, to keep balanced in every way, I have to relate also to others the same way. I can't relate to an associate merely from a business perspective. He has the same forces working on him—family decisions, peer-group pressure, social and emotional needs. In effect, I must look to his total being—something I don't always do.

The concept of wholeness relates to the maturing process. The term *well rounded* has the proper connotation. We're not to be lopsided. This happens in all areas. People often relate to only one of man's basic needs, whether it be physical, emotional, or spiritual. The Bible recognizes this, as it describes the need to relate to God with our minds, souls, and bodies.

Whole is beautiful! Strive for it. You will be wiser, happier, and healthier. Remember—the process is unending, as we mature to a wholesome wholeness.

Fulfillment

Our pastor, Earl Craig, today shared about the keys to fulfillment. Appropriately, he began by stressing the overriding concept of love as being required in order to have real fulfillment. He also shared that to have complete fulfillment, we need to learn to make decisions; we need to learn to adapt, to be honest; we need to have self-discipline; we need to be a team member; we need to get started.

I sense that you have personally discovered how to have fulfillment. Your mental self-discipline is a key ingredient. You act fulfilled! You never complain about lack of fulfillment! You have, I believe, made a key discovery in your life: fulfillment is possible—when we want it. This kind of fulfillment comes as we ask God to take control of our lives and as we draw on His great resources.

Never let the world tell you how to have the life of pleasure and that it can bring fulfillment. A full life comes only through God's perfect plan for us, and our yielding to the plan. Fulfillment is being a part of something beyond ourselves in which we've lost that basic selfish drive of man.

Worth

Most things have worth, or value, in the hands of the right person. Worth obviously then is relative—both as to location and specific circumstance. The economic concept of supply and demand determines, to a large degree, the worth of a particular commodity. Usefulness is another key for determining worth. A bottle opener has little intrinsic value, but it's worth a lot when really needed.

While things are assigned worth, we also tend to assign worth to people. We make value judgments: "He's worthless"; "She's

priceless"; "He's a worthy person." Even with people our usefulness comes into play. Are we someone of value to others? Do we
add or take away something when we're with others? Do we
bring a sense of joy, well-being, or do we cast gloom in our
paths?

Maximize your personal worth and be creative with others.
Give good value to life's interrelationships. I thank God for
those in my life who have real value and pass it on as they give to
others.

Value

For the past several days I've been working on the question of
what constitutes value. There are some temporary absolutes
where we can make nonnegotiated trades—dollars for German
marks or English pounds. Yet they change, too, as the market
changes.

Value depends on a myriad of things. One day a mood ring is
worth forty-five dollars and three weeks later, five dollars. It's
partially a matter of supply and demand. But it's also determined by the perspective of the person setting the value. Something might be priceless to me and of little value to someone else.
Intangibles come into play, such as sentiment.

To be successful in most businesses you must create a product
that is recognized generally as being of real value. The more
successful you are in convincing the public of the real value, the
more success you'll have.

There are some things of undefined value. No price tag can be
placed on them: honesty, truthfulness, fairness, concern. These
are the kinds of attributes for which to strive. They, in turn, will
create in you other characteristics of lasting value.

Duplication

I feel there's way too much duplication of effort. In a way, it's
not good stewardship. I enjoyed seeing a church in Henderson-
ville, North Carolina, where the church buildings were being

used on Saturdays by a Seventh-Day Adventist church and on Sundays by another church. I like to see this, even using our facilities for weekday activities such as craft classes or day-care centers.

Organizations are healthier when everyone understands his responsibility, and there's no overlap, no duplication. This is true in the business world, in the community, generally, and in our churches. This, then, enables everyone to fit together more effectively.

Duplication is wasteful. When I study a charity to which I'm considering contributing, I consider their unique contribution or whether it might just be a duplication of some other service being offered and there's no real need. I feel the key to service is to find that task that only *you* can do best—then do it. To be another "me, too" adds little excitement to our lives. So don't just be a duplicate; be an original.

Normal

Society does a lot to try to squeeze us into becoming "normal." To be out of the ordinary or special is frowned upon by many people. Don't buy it! Or at least don't buy what most people accept as normal. They accept the abnormal as being normal.

For example, the lackluster Christian life is viewed as normal. This is a device of Satan himself. Normal for the Christian life is really the life controlled by God's Holy Spirit—exciting and enthusiastic. Watchman Nee wrote the book *Normal Christian Life.* It describes much more than what most people accept as normal.

Most people perform at a pace less than what should be expected. They are considered normal. The problem is we've abnormally lowered our standards. Never be satisfied with the world's definition of what's normal performance. Set your standards based on God's requisites for you.

Discipline

One of the most important forces in molding our lives is discipline. It comes from forces both within ourselves and from others. Parental discipline should be designed to shape us into our full potential, but sometimes it fails. Discipline enforced by our society keeps us within a framework that provides order. It, too, sometimes fails.

I believe one of the most effective forms of discipline is that which is self-imposed. We have within ourselves the mental ability to discipline ourselves to achieve maximum results.

Accept discipline—from within and without. It will strengthen you. Learn to help discipline others. Don't fail others or yourself because of a lack of personal discipline in your life. Learn to be counted on.

Habits

We tend to become what we do on a constant basis. If we want to be a good worker, we learn to work. If we want to be a leader, we get in the habit of leading.

The word *habit* sometimes has a negative connotation. It leaves the impression that even good habits have no real merit. This idea can be a trap. Obviously, good physical habits protect our bodies and health. Spiritually speaking, we need to think out our activities and not just do things by rote. To go deeper in our relation to God, religion must be more than just habit.

Examine what you're doing. If good, continue it, even expand your effort. If bad, seek change in what you're doing. Overcome negative habits quickly. I've found it easy, but only when I absolutely made up my mind to do it. Develop good habits in study, health, and other areas that will build you up.

Life-style

Each of us develops a kind of life-style. It might be so evident to others that certain words are used to describe us: *uptight, loose, sincere, dedicated.* The things that determine our life-styles are the forces at work in our lives. Do I want to be like my mom or dad, or do I want to be unlike my mom or dad? Do I want to give some specific kind of appearance like Fonzie on TV, or do I just want to be myself?

To make the most of the joys in life, your life-style needs to be relaxed and natural. There should be no preconceived idea as to what you *have* to become or how successful you *have* to be financially.

The Bible tells of a life-style committed to God's leadership. This is the key to real peace—to *only* be what God wants us to be. I've seen so many people hurting because they sensed themselves being forced into a life-style by their peers, or their family, or their own idea of what a successful life is all about.

Again, be God's and be yourself. Ultimately, you need to please only Him—not me or anyone else. I look forward to continuing to see you grow into the life-style God has planned for you.

Pleasure

Man seeks pleasure in all his activities. Pleasure is the sense of well-being. We seek after physical pleasures, mental pleasures, and spiritual pleasures, or well-being. There's nothing wrong in pleasure. In fact, we should strive for it.

The real concern is that we find out quickly that self-seeking pleasures have no real lasting value. The ultimate pleasure in life is knowing that you're living it to the fullest extent possible, and that can be done only when you're within God's will. I believe the fantastic thing here is that God wants us to have more pleasure in life than we could ever dream possible.

The Book of Ecclesiastes zeroes in on how man seeks pleasure—through wisdom, women, wealth, wine. All are designed to appeal to man's base nature—that sense that we can please ourselves. The book ends with the answer: If we follow after God and His desire for us, we will gain more than would ever be possible in our own strengths. For the pleasures of life and eternity, we need to give ourselves over completely to God.

Fun

It's important to learn to have fun in life. Fun should be a natural by-product of many activities that we're involved in. We can develop an attitude that creates fun in all things—recreation, work, and all life's involvements.

Fun can be multiplied so that you create the same sense in others. Fun provides relaxation for our bodies and minds; so they can be used at a maximum level. Fun doesn't depend on things or special situations—it *is!*

Strive for fun in everything. It will provide great dividends, both physically and spiritually.

It's fun to discover new things. The most fun is finding the key to the full and abundant life in Christ.

Fitness

Physical fitness is really important for maximum enjoyment of life. Good physical fitness is a part of the stewardship of our lives. We owe it to ourselves, our families, and others to maintain ourselves with a high degree of fitness.

This week I received the results of my recent physical. Basically, the doctor rated me fair as to my physical fitness. He said I needed to lose weight and adjust my intake of beef. Although rather minor complaints, if taken care of, several years can be added to my life.

Fitness implies being trim—no excess baggage. This is important physically, but it's equally important psychologically. The same level of self-discipline is needed here to keep ourselves fit. Emotional and mental fitness also adds to being a well-rounded, healthy person.

Maintain a high level of fitness in all areas of your life—consistently. Don't let bad habits drag you down. Keeping alert to fitness goals will aid you tremendously in the years ahead.

Wages

I believe people are paid generally what they're worth. A man's wages usually follow his contribution to his company.

I've never had to ask for a raise; yet I've earned a lot of money. For the past twelve years, in both companies for which I've worked, I've received the largest bonus of any employee. It's not because I've sought it, but, rather, someone felt I earned it.

As a teenager, I earned more than all the other "bagboys." It was because half our earnings were tips; so I worked harder and faster to take out the most orders.

The key seems to me to be: Do such a good job that you will automatically be taken care of. Don't do enough to justify your pay but do so much more that your effort is recognized as being worth more than your pay.

No one owes you a living. You'll have to work for it. So decide early to do more than that required. You'll be the beneficiary.

Hiring

I'm in the process of trying to find a new secretary. The hiring process is an interesting one. To examine the comparative capabilities of different people and then to make a decision is very difficult.

The only time I've sought an employment opportunity since college was in 1957 when I went with the CPA firm of Ring, Mahoney, and Arner. I was offered a job after a short interview and have had no job interviews since that time. Firms have looked at my work effort and have made offers to me.

As I've interviewed people over the years, I've looked for these kinds of qualities: technical ability to get the job done, pleasing personality, and willingness to dedicate oneself to the total concepts of the company. I've never knowingly hired someone who just wanted to draw a paycheck.

In the future, as you consider various job possibilities, be sure to consider that you have to meet the needs of your employer. Nobody owes you a job. You earn the right through proper education and experience.

College

In several months, Valerie will be going off to college. In three years you will be going as well. Your years in college will be among the most important in your life. It will be your first long period of time away from home. You will be learning socially as well as intellectually.

The college you choose will have a real impact on what you become in the future. For Mom and me, our college days were like a supermarket. We took from the school what we needed but didn't let it sidetrack us from what we considered important in life. We continued to be very active in church life and most of our social activities centered there rather than in college groups.

Some colleges develop a real spirit among their students; some, even an intellectual snobbery. You can accomplish the most during your college years by selecting a school that will help prepare you as a well-rounded person. A good college life addresses itself to the total man—not just the social, nor just the intellectual, but, rather, to every aspect of your being.

Education

The moment we're born we begin to learn. The process is never over, even though at times in our lives the process is easier and more natural. You are at that time in your life now, so take advantage of it and learn all you can. Use what you learn now and also build on it for the effect it will have in the future.

Education is a broad term. It encompasses the formal learning achieved through schooling as well as knowledge gained through assimilation. Your formal education is very important to your future. It will help form life's goals. It will give you more than information and knowledge. You will gain self-confidence and poise.

Education should be a high priority in your life at your age. Later this priority will change, but you will maximize your personal potential if you will never be satisfied with what you know. Let the educational process broaden you to the maximum extent. You will be thankful throughout life.

Accountability

**God's stewardship requires that we give our-
selves completely—everything that we have
and everything that we are.**

Example

You are an example! You've heard it many times, as I have; yet I'm reminded of it constantly. People write letters, telling me how something I said or did had an impact on their lives. One employee said in a very personal note that he had a new hero.

We might not even want to be an example; yet it happens. It's not of our choosing. We have to ask these basic questions: What if everyone talked the way I do or sang the way I sing or had the enthusiasm that I have?

You must be especially careful in setting an example for your peers and those younger than you. At R.A. Camp those young kids will be watching everything you do. After all, you're their leader. Take real care of your influence on others.

Also, select carefully those whose examples you follow. I've selected men such as Arthur Blessitt, the evangelist whose unconventional witness takes him to rock concerts, Times Square, and pornography shops; Reid Hardin, director of lay renewal for the Home Mission Board of our Southern Baptist Convention; and Charles Kellstadt, who is now deceased but was the president of Sears, Roebuck and Co. They have qualities within them that I want to emulate. Of course, ultimately my model is Christ—the perfect example.

Responsibility

I'm reminded today of a responsibility I have as teacher of my Sunday-school class. The responsibility is mine. The church asked me to accept it. I evaluated whether I should; prayed about it; then accepted it.

Now, in the carrying out of my responsibility, it is incumbent on me to discover how to do the best possible job. One of the ways is to be effective in my teaching. I've been adequate here.

Another thing I could do is to get to know the men on a more personal basis. Here, I've done very poorly. Another way is to encourage fellowship. We're doing that tonight in a class party.

Our responsibilities are varied. Some are absolute such as my responsibility to you as a father; others are optional such as my accepting the teaching role in a Sunday-school class. Because they are many and varied, we need to constantly remind ourselves of them.

You have a number of responsibilities. Identify them and be sensitive in meeting them. It requires a high degree of self-discipline for you to stay on top of them. Yet the satisfaction is well worth it. We grow through the execution of life's responsibilities.

Accountability

We're all accountable to some person or group of persons. I'm accountable to my superior; he, in turn, to another senior officer; he, to the president; he, to the board of directors; and the directors, to the stockholders; and even the stockholders, to the public and its welfare.

As an accountant, I think I understand the concept of accountability. It relates to time, effort, and results. It involves the question: "What have I done with the resources given me?" The Bible teaches accountability in the parable of the talents.

The toughest person to whom I'm accountable is myself. I set goals, and I know how hard I've worked to achieve them or how slack I've been. I target results, and if I don't make them, I try to analyze why. I then resolve to overcome the problems or disciplines of the past; so I won't be short in the next accounting.

Of course, ultimately, I'm accountable to God. He has given me all I have. It's my responsibility to use it wisely and to return to Him, as a faithful steward, the fruit of living a life dedicated to serving Him.

Managers

One of my pet peeves is managers who don't manage. This past week I saw an example of both a good manager and one not so strong. The first one came up with the solution to a company problem. He researched it, analyzed it thoroughly, discussed it with all the appropriate people, wrote up the procedure that answered the need, and then implemented it. It wasn't easy. He pushed hard to clarify the company's position. He even pushed me, and he got the job done. I sent him a note commending him for his work.

At least in two other cases, I worked with managers who were approaching their jobs halfheartedly. They would take a matter to a point and then kick it to me. I received a forty-one page report absolutely full of numbers but with no analysis of what all these numbers meant. Nor was there an indication as to what was being done about the situations where the numbers indicated less than projected performance. While I can determine a proper course of action, the person submitting the report should be in a position to provide some direction.

When you're in a managerial role, you must be adept at pinpointing a problem, searching out solutions, summarizing data, and recommending and implementing solutions.

Ethics

I read an address today by the president of a major company. He said that "perhaps the principal issue before the international business community this year is the question of worldwide business conduct."

As a member of my company's Corporate Ethics Committee, I've studied the positions of a number of companies and thought out some of the problems. It's serious. Every day we see where business, political, or even religious leaders have succumbed to the pressure of a mixed-up society as it relates to personal or corporate ethics.

One of the tests of ethical conduct we discussed was this: Never ask an employee to do something he doesn't feel comfortable doing from an ethical standpoint. It's not cut-and-dried. A Christian perspective helps, but more is needed. I believe the answer lies in spiritual discernment. In other words, what is right in a given situation (not situation ethics) can be discerned through a sense of divine direction. I know when I pray about some decision that has to be made, I have a better feel for what's ethically right.

Standards

There are all kinds of standards: standards of conduct, standards of living, standards of morality. In fact, there are standards that affect every area of our lives. Some are forced on us by government, some by our culture or society, some by our family and friends, and others by ourselves.

Valerie wrote to our congressman about the new metric-system legislation to express her views on this standard of measurement. She's right. We ought to examine carefully both the standards imposed on us and those we set for ourselves. They affect every aspect of our lives.

You are now, and will be to a greater extent in the future, a standard setter. Standards need to be set, or accepted, with care. Today one of our employees didn't want to accept a standard of performance established by our company, yet it is a proper one, and we must live by it.

Set your own standards high and let them be progressive in nature. Let them really challenge the way you live. Obviously, the number-one standard setter is God Himself. Follow His standards.

Utilization

The proper utilization of our resources fits well into my concept of reaching our potentials as individuals, as a nation, and as a world. We "underutilize" or "misutilize" our vast resources which could bring more personal happiness as well as material well-being.

I read where Brazil has sufficient timber to build a home for every family in existence. Yet this resource is going virtually untapped while Japanese homes are being built with pressed paper made from pulp wood.

Utilization isn't something to be thought of only when considering natural resources but also personal resources. Each of us has certain inherent or God-given capabilities. The degree that they're utilized will determine the level of personal success. And this relates to all areas of life, not just the material.

The degree to which you and I use talents, gifts, and abilities sets the stage for that sense of accomplishment for a job well done. We know if it's happening. If there's any question, God's Spirit will give us the degree of discernment we need.

Learn to utilize all available resources. It's good stewardship. It brings a sense of fulfillment.

Stewardship

Today we're practicing stewardship. We are flying halfway across the country to share the Good News of Jesus Christ with an entire church body.

First, it's stewardship of our time. I've taken a day of my vacation, and you've taken off from school so that we can help coordinate this lay-renewal weekend. I believe it's a good use of our time—thus good stewardship.

Second, it requires stewardship of our finances since we paid for six of those attending the weekend. Again, the dollars mean little when compared to the anticipated results.

Third, it involves stewardship of all our other resources— spiritual, physical, and mental. Sunday afternoon we'll be pretty tired and drained. The intensity is great. But I'm sure it will be worth all the effort.

Good stewardship requires that we give ourselves completely—everything we have and everything we are—to our task. In this case, I have no doubt that God will give the increase to both those to whom we minister and to us.

Source

As you observe life and all its involvements, be careful to note the source of those things that would influence you. A mighty river has a very small insignificant source, yet consider its impact. A word from a special source means much more than simply casual expression.

As I get certain mail and note the source, it automatically is discarded. I know the source is unreliable. Yet I devour information received from others. The same is true of speakers. I weigh carefully not only what's said but the source from which it comes.

You are a source for others. Be careful what you pass on. You never know who or how it might influence others. As you receive from other sources, sort it out and pass on that which would be beneficial to others.

You not only are a source of information, but also a source of inspiration. No one can lift me higher than you at those critical times when you pray for me or inspire me by just being yourself.

Edify

People need strengthening on a regular basis. To help others through building them up is to edify. This is a gift which the Bible teaches that God gives to some people. While some exercise this gift with a real degree of success, many of us never realize our potential to help others.

I'm constantly surprised at how much I can lift a person's spirits with a positive word. I have also noted how a simple word, or a look, can be devastating to a person's ego or mood.

Since we have such tremendous influence over the attitudes and spiritual well-being of others, we need to be careful to build them up—to edify. Isn't this a good investment—very little effort on our part but fantastic return in the lives of others?

Also recognize the gift of edification in others as they relate to you or as you ask them to counsel with a third party. Realize that others affect you and be thankful for it and your responsibility to be a positive force on others.

Influence

Today we visited a church where I had the opportunity to speak at the worship service. I'm thankful that I had this chance to share. I know God can use our individual influences to affect other people. A number of people shared after the service how they had recommitted their lives to Christ. I thank God for that.

I've sensed in a number of good, strong Christian people the fear of using their personal influence to share the Good News of Christ. This is a tremendous waste. People are constantly making decisions that affect their lives. If we can influence them, under the leadership of the Holy Spirit, then we can't pass up that opportunity. In fact, it's more than an opportunity; it's a responsibility. You have influence, so guard it carefully. Use it to strengthen others for good. Be careful not to influence others adversely, because we will be held accountable.

Movies

Today we saw a good spy movie. The only thing wrong with it was the selection of some pretty bad words. While I know they're not new to your hearing, their repetition brings us to the point of greater acceptance. So we need to avoid as much as possible exposing ourselves to this kind of language.

Movies and TV do have a real influence on our lives: how we dress; how we act; and even how we think. I've seen several movies I wish I had never seen, because I sense the influence they have on my thought process. While I ask God to keep my mind positive and under His influence, it becomes easier if my mind isn't cluttered with filth.

You need to be very selective in the movies you choose to see. This will become even more important as you grow older, especially as you begin to date. Then you'll not only be influencing yourself, but someone else as well. Select carefully.

Owe

My Sunday-school lesson today was on the subject, "What Do I Owe God?" As I thought about this, my mind ran to what I owe others as well as God. What do I owe my mother for raising all five of us kids and giving us the basis for a life in Christ? How much do I owe your mom for sharing my life, making it complete, and for those little things like encouraging me to go on in my education, even enrolling me in college?

What do I owe you or Valerie for all the joy you've brought into my life? Or what do I owe men like Bob Hudson, our friend from Florida who is visiting with us today, for initiating us into a new life-style in which we sense God's direction? What do I owe Reid Hardin, or Dr. John Haldeman and Dr. Culbreth, two of our former pastors, or Arthur Blessitt and on and on down the list which I could go?

Yes, we owe a lot to others, and we ought to reflect on it periodically. We ought to thank those who have had a big impact on our lives and those who continue to impact us each day. And, of course, each day we ought to thank God for what He's done for us. We owe Him so much. He paid such a price for us, and I'm thankful for all of it.

Duty

There is inherent in man's responsibility a concept of duty, or obligation. Duty connotes a definite assignment or role in a particular situation. There's no getting away from it—even though often it's something you want to avoid.

As a father, I have specific duties to you. Some of them are set by our culture—some of them even by law—but I think the most important are those assigned to me by God.

In a similar way you have duties. They will change over the years. I am probably guilty of not giving you sufficient duties. I say *guilty* because the execution of one's various duties helps to mature a person. The more duties we have, the more we grow. Therefore, I ought to assign you more specific projects to accomplish.

Become aware of those inherent duties you have as a son, a brother, a Christian, a student, and a citizen.

Worship

Worship is "giving worth" to something or someone. The assigning of value or worth should be done very carefully. By misplacing value, we can easily lose the real joy in life. You can see it all around you—people assigning real value to money, position, material possessions, and on and on.

Learn to evaluate properly what has real value. Ultimate

worth comes only from God and His infinite direction. This means we should really worship only God Himself. Then we have things in proper perspective.

Worship is accomplished through prayer, meditation, giving praise, study, and even serving God. Whatever we do that gives worth or assigns value to our relationship to God is worship. There's no limitation as to time, place, or method. Learn to worship effectively. It will strengthen your life.

Emptiness

Man without God is empty—no matter the degree of human success he's managed to achieve. Recently I've met several multimillionaires who are searching, who acknowledge that all is for naught. One man said with his hundreds of millions of dollars, he couldn't get a single member of his family to go to a movie with him, after trying for several weeks.

Life needs never to be empty. It can be full of all kinds of exciting activities as well as a sense of comfort and well-being. Even Christians lead lives that, if not totally empty, do not have the fullness available to them.

Being a problem solver by nature, I ask, "Why?" It's because many people don't know the "how" to a full life, and with others, ego gets in the way. So our job, as possessors of the Good News, is to share it—not just to tell others that we have it but how they can enjoy all the blessings God has for them.

Courtesy

There's a basic courtesy due every person. It should become automatic that we treat others properly. It should be natural and not something we have to work at. When someone does something special for us, we owe them a special note of courtesy.

One of the keys to being courteous is to have a feeling of respect for others. If we respect a person, then we will tend to be more courteous to him. This doesn't mean that we act one way to those we know and respect highly, but, rather, that we learn to respect everyone.

Feigned courtesy means little. You and Val have pointed out how some people act one way in a person's presence and then put them down when they're no longer present. Again, it's important to be real in our actions, which means we must feel them.

Courtesy isn't always easy, because another person is involved, and his actions might not invite a positive response. Yet it's something you owe him. It doesn't change based on the actions of others. Being courteous will strengthen your life and make your relationships more meaningful.

Honest

Sometimes it's hard to be absolutely honest in all things, particularly when being honest will hurt others. Sometimes I find myself doing things for others that I don't have the time or energy to do, but I hate to say no to them. I guess it would be best to go ahead and tell them my deep inner feelings in as pleasant a way as possible and then move on to something else.

I heard someone say last week that it's difficult to be honest in business. That's nonsense! Honesty is wrapped up in the concept of fairness: a fair price, a fair return on investment, a fair quality and quantity. We can be fair and honest and still make a good profit for our company.

Be honest in your word—it represents your inner being.
Be honest in your dealings with others—it will be reciprocated.
Be honest in evaluating your own effort—the gain will be great.
Be honest in deed and thought—it will make you a more complete person.

Reason

The ability to reach a proper conclusion through reason separates a few from most of us. The majority don't want to bother to reason things out. They jump to the conclusions that impress them. Usually man will seek the answer that fits his purpose. We forget reason for the sake of our own selfish purposes.

To reason is to consider every facet of a situation, to get the maximum input, to sort it out, and to let develop an overall sense of rightness. To consider only ourselves and our feelings is not reason; it's merely selfishness.

We use reasons to set our courses of action. Because this is true, we need to be sure the reasons have been reasoned out. To accept false or improper premises will lead to improper actions or conclusions on our part. This basic fact is demonstrated in the syllogistic reasoning process in logic. A premise such as "Anything I do to gain financial success is okay" can lead to havoc in our lives. On the other hand, a decision such as "I will do what I sense God wants me to do in my life" will lead to a life full of happiness.

Gambling

I visited the gambling center of the world today—Las Vegas. While we were going to look at new types of housing—virtually every other person on our plane was going to Las Vegas to gamble. There's a carnival atmosphere in town, and money and morals are loose. You could easily get caught up in the frenzied pace.

Gambling is obviously not good financial stewardship. To lose several hundreds, or thousands, of dollars is an absolute waste. The gambling fever has broken up homes and families. One man on our plane bragged about flying out from Dallas on the spur of the moment, over the strong objection of his wife.

There's technically no way to beat the system. It's based on chance, or at least that's what they contend. You can be highly trained at figuring the odds and still have to admit that the odds are against you. The house must ultimately win.

You have a fine financial mind. Don't ever let it get side-tracked with gambling. It hurts others, and it hurts you. In the long run, there is no winner. Therefore be a good steward of your financial means.

Insurance

One of the things with which I've had a problem in the past is knowing how much insurance to carry on my life for the benefit of Mom, Valerie, and you.

Insurance should not be bought just to create wealth for those left behind but rather for their protection until the children have reached their earning potential and have established their own homes.

Sometime I'd like to go over my insurance program with you and fully explain it. It also fits into my will which we can also discuss. Of course, the key protection is for your mother. She needs to be provided with sufficient support; so she can be independent of requiring help from both you and Valerie. As we study this together, you can get an idea of what you need to do about insurance in the future.

Money

One of the most useful economic tools is money, but, remember, it's only a tool to be used and not an end in itself!

Money should be respected—not loved!
It should be earned—not greedily sought!
It should be used as an economic force for good—not evil!
Money can help make us better people—or it can destroy us.

God requires of us a stewardship of all we have—money and all other possessions, both tangible and intangible. Learn to give more than that required. It will bring its own reward. Learn to budget your financial resources.

Never let money control you. Be in constant control of yourself under God's leadership.

Strive to earn to your potential and then use the financial rewards carefully.

Weight

I've been very conscious of my weight lately. The doctor wants me to lose fifteen pounds in the next three months. It's going to require a lot of self-discipline—and God's help. With me, it's also going to require an adjustment in my basic diet.

Valerie is good about watching her weight. Her everyday weigh-in is almost a ritual with her. Mom's weight has been almost constant from her teenage years. You're in good shape now, and by the end of the summer, you'll be in better shape.

Maintaining your weight and physical shape is a part of your stewardship. I've found I can do less for God in direct proportion to my weight going up. Carrying all that excess weight is a drain on available strength.

You have fair habits now to control your weight. Keep them—even improve them—and you'll do better in school. You'll have better relationships with your friends, including possible dates. The fact is, you'll just enjoy life more.

Exercise

Today we're beginning our exercise program. Again we see the need for discipline in our lives. Exercise is something that we should do throughout life.

It's especially important to you now, since you will be in a competitive situation at school, where it's important for you to be strong and vigorous.

Exercise is stimulating from a physical-health standpoint, but it goes beyond that. Physical health affects our mental and emotional health, and all three affect our spiritual health. Of course, we need to exercise ourselves directly in these other areas as well.

You are in good shape physically. Be thankful for that and maintain your body as a part of life's stewardship.

Our Country

You and I enjoy an unusual heritage. We are a part of the greatest nation that ever existed. We need to think about it, recognize it, enjoy it and thank God for it.

America is the way it is because of its people. They are diverse, from many backgrounds, but there's an unusual unity that binds them together. I feel democracy, tied into theocracy, is man's only hope—the people, ruling democratically, under the umbrella of God's direction. Man is limited; so our only hope for maximum good is to seek God's leadership in all we do. "Seek ye first the kingdom of God . . . and all these things shall be added unto you" (Matthew 6:33).

We can never forget that we have a tremendous responsibility for what America is. It's a stewardship—a trust from almighty God. I'm a part of it! You're a part of it! Be faithful in your loyalty to our great nation—America, the Beautiful.

Poison

Our pastor, Dr. Craig, shared today on the subject, "There's Poison in the Melting Pot." His Memorial Day message centered on what made America great and the poisons that are weakening our greatness. The message wasn't negative, but, rather, a message that challenged us to consider the poisons and to beware of their effects. He stressed there's time to correct the situation.

The poisons he described include the idea that big government can solve all our problems. He also warned of insipid socialism and the moral deterioration of our society. Each of these is a valid concern.

The hope for America rests in a renewal of the American spirit. Just as God purified the poisonous pot in 2 Kings 4:41, He can purify America. The way to purify America is to cleanse ourselves—Americans. It must begin with the church—God's people—then we can be effective vessels to be used by God to win our nation to our Creator and Saviour.

Taxes

It's been said that only two things are certain—death and taxes. We pay fantastic amounts of our incomes in taxes. Some are direct, and some, indirect. The direct ones include real-estate tax, income tax, and sales tax. The indirect taxes that we pay are those included in the price we pay for merchandise.

Taxes can be regressive in nature and hurt those with the least ability to pay, such as the sales tax on life's necessities. Or they can be progressive in nature—that is, they increase at a percentage as the base is increased—such as our federal income tax.

I've never minded paying taxes. After all, it's for services rendered to me and my family. I do, however, hate to see the terrible waste. I believe we could simplify our federal income-tax structure. It could be made fairer without so many loopholes, making it harder for some to avoid paying.

War

During my lifetime, our country has been involved in three major wars: World War II, the Korean War, and the war in Vietnam. The impact of these wars on our lives is hard to estimate, but it's fantastically big in the cost in lives, in wasted energy, in wasted national resources.

We can hope that mankind has seen the futility of war; yet,

historically speaking, that's a big hope. Can you imagine what would happen to our world in an all-out nuclear war? It's too horrible to even consider. We need to pray that it will never happen.

I also hope that you never have to go off to war to help protect your country. But if you do, I know you would be a good soldier, because you have many of the characteristics needed. You are mentally alert, physically strong, and have a willingness to be part of a team. All these are needed by the good soldier.

Press

Yesterday we had a press conference in which I shared our company's plans to introduce a new housing line. It was great. The mayor attended, business leaders, community leaders, about fifty people, and, of course, the press.

I've been astonished at the power of the press. If they desire, they can take what's said and twist it to accomplish their purposes. Most of the reporters were fair and objective. One wanted to zero in on his negative feelings toward the housing industry.

In the past when I've talked to reporters from national newspapers, I've often found a real lack of concern for truth. If they can sensationalize the news by giving only half-truths, many times this is the road they take. Obviously, all reporters don't fall into this breed.

Since freedom of the press is so important to our way of life, we must work at preserving it. At the same time we must hold those responsible who distort the news and use the press only as a means to accomplish their selfish purposes.

Environment

Environment is a word which has had accelerated use in the past ten years. Man has become more and more conscious of the need to protect his environment. From this standpoint I'm an environmentalist. A problem has developed, though, with those who are concerned with our aesthetic environment but are unwilling to consider the impact of our total environmental picture, including the social and economic consequences.

Environmental controls have related costs such as a landowner denied the use of his land or a business infrastructure becoming unbalanced because of cost constraints. If there must be control to protect ourselves, that's fine. The problem comes when we jump in and don't count the cost. The legislative danger is that states and the United States Congress might act for strictly political reasons rather than for our common good.

Spiritually speaking, God made us stewards of His creation. Today this requires the wisdom of a Solomon and can't be turned over to special interest groups on either side of the environmental issue. Wise men and women can tackle this national problem and come to sound conclusions without having to take adversary positions.

Faith

You have **no assurance from the indifferent;**
you sense an assurance from your friends; you
are satisfied of the assurance from those who
love you, but you can have absolute assurance
in your perfect Maker and Saviour—Jesus
Christ.

Man

A very mixed-up friend told me, "Man is his own god. You're god; I'm god." Yet as his self-made god, he leads the most frustrating kind of existence. He searched for truth but was unwilling to accept the simplicity of God's plan for his life.

Man is only man. We cannot make ourselves gods. God's Word says, "You shall have no other gods before me" (Exodus 20:3 RSV). This includes treating life as though we are adequate to control it ourselves.

It is important to recognize that God created man and that He gave man a uniqueness among all creation. He made us in His *image* but not from His mold. He breathed into us a fantastic potential, which we can use for good or, if we elect, evil.

Man must also recognize his limitations. As much as I might love someone, I cannot pay the price for his eternal salvation, nor can I give him a sense of love or joy or peace. But Christ, who lives within me, can reach out to others, touch their lives, and change them—transform them into new people. I recognize my "manness" and ask God to draw me closer to Him; so I can be more of what He wants me to be.

Lifesavers

I love Lifesavers—all kinds, all flavors. But have you thought about the real lifesavers? Ultimately, there is only one Lifesaver. That is Jesus Christ. We change His description from Saver to Saviour—both words fit His ultimate purpose.

While I'm not a lifesaver, I can share with others the Lifesaver I have.

Linda's life was saved, because I shared my Lifesaver!
Mr. Gonzalez, the taxi driver, is a Christian, because I told him of my Lifesaver!

My army buddy is a Christian brother, since I told him of
    my Lifesaver.
The black guard knows Jesus personally, because I told
    him of my Lifesaver.

Our Lifesaver gives more than a brief good taste. He fills my
life constantly with real love, peace, and joy. He flavors my life
with a real zest for living. The sweet taste of Jesus *lasts* and *lasts*.
    While we have a beautiful Life*saver*, we also enjoy a Life*shaper*
and a *New-life Maker*. Our Lifesaver is all this and more.

Assurance

There are many things of which I can't be sure: my business
connections, the stock market, the political scene, people's actions. But there's one thing of which I'm absolutely certain: God
will keep *every one* of His precious promises.

I have an assurance of my personal salvation, because
    God's Word tells me: ". . . Believe on the Lord Jesus
    Christ, and thou shalt be saved . . ." (Acts 16:31).
I have an assurance of a cleansed life, because He prom-
    ised me I could be holy and pure.
I have an assurance of love, joy, and peace in my life,
    because God promises me these attributes when I
    give myself over to the control of the Holy Spirit.

It's good to be sure of something. It's a comfortable feeling. I
have this feeling each day, because I have experienced the reality of this assurance.
    You have no assurance from the indifferent; you sense an
assurance from your friends; you are satisfied of the assurance
from those who love you, but you can have absolute assurance in
your perfect Maker and Saviour—Jesus Christ.

Faith

Over and over again we hear sermons on faith. Faith is basic in our relationship to God through Jesus Christ. As a monk believing in the concept of Christian works, Martin Luther discovered the truth of man's relationship to God: ". . . The just shall live by faith" (Romans 1:17; Galatians 3:11).

Faith is the beginning point. While it's basic, and continuing, it becomes easier to have faith as we mature as Christians. It's easier now for me to have faith, because I've experienced the results of faith. In effect, I take the first step in faith, and God then undergirds my effort and demonstrates His desired intimacy with me.

The great men of all time are those who had a high degree of faith. In the Bible we see men like Abraham and Paul. In history we see men like Abraham Lincoln, whose faith saved our United States. Great men have always demonstrated faith; the greatest have demonstrated faith in God. Faith in our own efforts is useless. Faith even in our nation, while worthy, is temporary, but faith in God will bring eternal results for us, individually and as a nation.

Our Risen Lord

On Easter we celebrate an absolute fact: We don't serve a philosopher, great teacher, prophet, or founder of a religion; rather, we serve the *Risen* Lord—Jesus Christ.

Whether the time for Easter—or Christmas, either—coincides with the times of Jesus' Resurrection and birth is not important. The ultimate importance rests in the *fact* of these occurrences.

Easter is a time when we can reconsider God's perfect plan for man's salvation—how Jesus paid the penalty for all our sins. God's plan didn't end there, but, rather, in Christ's victory over death—demonstrated historically in the fact of His Resurrection.

Just as Jesus has a new life beyond His physical death, we, too, as followers of Christ, have assurance of this same perfect new life. So, we can constantly celebrate this freshness and newness—even now. Paul said in his writing, "I have been crucified with Christ: and I myself no longer live, but Christ lives in me . . ." (Galatians 2:20 LB). We have this same assurance. Christ is in us. Therefore, it's a great day to celebrate!

Jesus

This week while Arthur Blessitt has been visiting with us, I have taken him around to share with various groups. As he spoke to one group he emphasized something we tend to forget as Christians—the fact that the best picture of what the Christian should be is not found in the teachings of the epistles, but rather in the life of Jesus.

A book that affected me as a teenager was the book *In His Steps* by Charles Sheldon. It asks the basic question that will answer man's search for God's will in a specific situation: "What would Jesus do?" It's Jesus we should use as our model—not our parents, friends, pastor, or other biblical characters.

We should spend more time studying the life of Christ and sensing how He reacted to the people He met and the problems He saw. We can also learn from His prayer life.

We know who Jesus was and is. We do need to let Him become in us everything He wants to become.

Discipleship

More than anything else in the world, I want you to have that intimate, intense relationship with Jesus Christ that comes from giving yourself completely to Him. To put it in another way: Seek to become a faithful disciple of Christ in all you do.

I believe this is where joy comes in life—from serving God in everything. Never get the idea this is for "someday." It's for now!

Discipleship is a two-way street. You are discipled by those around you, and you in turn disciple others. You're ministered to, and you minister.

This is a basic part of life's journey—the development of a life-style that accomplishes God's purpose through you. Don't wait. Let God work His purpose now!

Testimony

Your testimony is yours alone! No one else can share exactly what you share. We've just been through a lay renewal where you heard many people share their testimonies. Some share matter-of-factly, while others share with more emotion. There's no proper way to share your testimony. The key is to tell *your* story and not to use a testimony as a time to preach.

The reason we have testimony sharing in our lay-renewal activities is to verbally demonstrate that most of us have the same kinds of joys, that we all hurt some, and that frustration is not unusual. But hopefully it goes beyond this. It also relates to how we've found some answers to life's problems—not necessarily *all* the answers, but some.

A testimony, to be effective, needs to be up-to-date—what's happening in my life today! It's a way to share a little of yourself. Most people are interested in you and what you have to say; so always be ready to share yourself with others.

Holiness

God gave each of us the ability to stand pure and holy before Him. From a human standpoint, it's hard to imagine that we could have these qualities which are assigned to God, but we can—through God Himself.

God's Word says we are ". . . a royal priesthood, an holy nation, a peculiar people . . ." (1 Peter 2:9). This is another of those precious promises of the Bible.

As a young man, dare to be different; lean heavily on God's forgiveness and the cleansing power that God provided through His Son, Jesus Christ.

You have Christ in your life—the holiest man who ever walked among men. You, too, can have this same holiness—if you seek after Him and His forgiving power.

Good

The Bible teaches: "There is none good but one" (*see* Luke 18:19). From experience we know that this is a fact. The natural question, then, is: "Is there any hope for us to be 'good'?" By man's definition we might say yes. We say, "He's a good man." But the *good* referred to in this verse implies a righteousness. Can I really be all that God intends—in my own strength? The answer is no. But there is a way for us to enjoy God's goodness—by possessing Jesus Christ in our lives.

The only real good I can accomplish is by letting Christ be released through my life. I did this several days ago at the state school with the kids there. I believe they sensed God's love—through me.

When I become personally defeated, I know that I've not let God's goodness flow easily in my life. As I take time to think out my problem and meditate and pray, I sense His perfect will and I feel a mental restoration.

You are good because you have God in your life. I see that goodness over and over again. I also see the need, in both you and me, to be broken from self-will and to let God's goodness flow.

Immortality

Man is the only immortal creation of God. Genesis 1:27 says, "So God created man in his own image . . . ." Man is unique in this respect—God "fashioned our hearts" (*see* Psalms 33:15). The immortality of man—the fact that our souls will live on after our earthly death—places on us a fantastic responsibility.

Man can choose to bind himself to God to live in eternity as a son of God, or he can choose to turn away from God with the consequence of eternal separation from God's goodness.

Our immortal nature is absolutely sealed! We've accepted God's plan of restoring ourselves to Him through His Son, Jesus Christ. Now the question is this: What are we to do for our fellow man? Without Christ he is absolutely doomed. Our task, then, is to share Christ and His perfect redemptive plan with all men. If we fail in this, we've sealed that man's immortal nature to hell— eternal separation from God.

Recognize your own immortality, and that of all mankind, and act accordingly. You can affect where someone spends eternity.

Salvation

Personal salvation is the most important thing in life for us to understand. The sad thing is that many people do not have the faintest idea how they can be saved. One pastor responded to Arthur Blessitt's question: "Are you saved?" by replying, "Saved from what?" We know salvation as a means whereby man, acknowledging his sin and separation from God, accepts Jesus Christ to bridge that gap—to become his personal Saviour. Because it's accomplished by personal faith rather than something we gain through our effort, many never find it.

Inherent in the idea of salvation is the concept of reconciliation—to be brought into balance with God's intended purpose for our lives. Because of the adequacy of the price paid for my salvation through Jesus Christ, nothing further is required. I have it for eternity.

A beautiful aspect of salvation is the availability of a maturing, healthy relationship with God. This door is open to me. I can draw as close to God as my faith allows and thus enjoy the beautiful journey begun in salvation.

Revelation

Today in my Sunday school we talked about the concept of how God revealed Himself to man. I believe strongly in the idea of "progressive revelation"—that is, God revealed Himself to man on a more detailed basis progressively throughout history. The key is that the "ultimate revelation" of God was in the person of Jesus Christ.

Someone asked the question: How can we know we have God's total revelation of Himself when it was progressive in nature for so long? My answer was, when God became man and demonstrated the perfect life in Christ, what more could He reveal?

I do believe that you and I can, on a progressive basis, know more and more about Christ. This is spiritual growth—maturing in our relation to Him. James 4:8 says, "When you draw close to God, God will draw close to you" (LB). So if we want God revealed more effectively in our lives, then we must draw close to Him to mature, to become whole, to be complete.

God's Will

You've heard me say many times that God's Word teaches that God has a perfect will for our lives. While He has this perfect plan for us, it's only offered, not forced upon us. We have the option of accepting or rejecting it.

I believe we can tell when we're within God's will. It's clear that God teaches us that we're to be empowered and controlled by the Holy Spirit. God's Word also teaches that when this happens, we're producing the fruit of the Spirit—love, joy, peace, and so on. Therefore, it follows that if we're within His will, we have peace in our lives. It's also a good test to acknowledge that if we don't have that peace, we need to seek God's leadership in our lives.

The journey we're on is exciting when we know for certain that we're doing what God wants us to do. Strive for this sense of being 100 percent within God's will. It's great!

Prayer

Prayer is one of the strongest forces in life. Prayer can bring miracles. Prayer can bring us close to God. Prayer is a means of expressing thanks. Prayer gives us an opportunity to share the most intimate need with God.

Discipline yourself to pray regularly, not out of habit, but because of the constancy of our needs and thankfulness. Learn to talk to God freely when you're happy, sad, perplexed, or even when you're unaware of what's happening in your life.

Prayer is cleansing, refreshing, exhilarating! Prayer gives us a series of new beginnings. Pray for anything and for everything. Prayer is fellowship—with almighty God. Don't miss it. Enjoy it.

Answers

To some questions there are no adequate answers. My basic nature wants to find the answer. Yet, I've learned to accept that for which I cannot discover the answer. This requires faith in our lives.

In a spiritual sense, we especially want God to give us direct answers to our prayers. Yet, it's been appropriately said:

When the *request* is not right, God says no!
When the *time* is not right, God says slow!
When *I* am not right, God says grow!
When *everything* is right, God says go!

Generally, we don't like this waiting. We want to know *now*. For example, I'd like to know if we made a good investment this week when we went "short" in a stock option. We'll have our answer, but maybe not for a month or more.

In the religious area, why is there so much disagreement? Some claim to have *the* answer. Yet others refute this claim with their *own* answer. For me, I'll be satisfied when I ultimately find *all* the answers, and that will happen when I go to be with *The Answer.*

To seek answers for those problems and questions that are answerable is fun. Yet I have to admit I don't have all the answers. This, too, is no problem—discovery adds an exciting dimension to life.

Meditation

I've always wondered how people find time for personal meditation—at least in a block of time. I'm more and more aware of the need for it in my life. I've always prayed—constantly throughout the day—but never had a formal plan.

Today I began to use the *Spiritual Daybook,* a daily diary of one's spiritual life, published by Ras Robinson and Jesse McElreath, consultants in discipleship ministries. I believe it's going to help me be more disciplined in my meditation. It forces us to a regimen that's good for us.

I believe through meditating about God's will and seeking Him and His direction that we can move forward in our Christian walk. I'm definitely not satisfied with my relationship to Christ. I want the something more that Jack Taylor shares in his book *Much More* and that God promises in His Book.

You already do a lot of thinking. This is fine. But convert some of that thinking time to periods of meditation when you consider God and the perfection He plans for you. I'm going to enjoy growing closer to God, through Christ, in the power of the Holy Spirit by means of times of personal meditation.

Christmas

Today is the most important holiday within the Western world. People relate to the holiday season in many different ways. For some it's strictly economic. Some retail businesses make as much as half their annual sales in December. To others it's a time to renew our commitment to the One whose birth we are celebrating—Jesus Christ.

While we acknowledge that Jesus' birth was probably at a different time of year and that Christianity adopted the date of a Roman holiday, I see little significance to all this. The key to me, any year, is that God's Son, Jesus Christ, was born and He lived and was a living revelation of God Himself. Then He died to pay the penalty for all mankind's sins. This is what we should celebrate—the joy of God's total purpose in the coming of Christ.

Never take lightly the beauty of this holiday season. Always use it to reconfirm your allegiance to Christ and to others. It's a special family time—to our family, to our larger family of aunts, uncles, grandparents, and then to all those in the family of God. Show God's love to all of these at this special time of year.

Holy Spirit

We believe in the triune God—the three-fold nature of God. While our finite minds have a hard time fully understanding infinite God, I believe we can grasp, in lay terms, the realities concerning God.

The Holy Spirit is God. The work of the Holy Spirit is to convict us of our sins and to convince us of the rightness of God's perfect plan for our lives.

As long as we're sensitive to the working of the Holy Spirit in our lives, we will sense this convicting and His convincing. God doesn't impose Himself on man. Therefore, we have this intense or intimate relationship only as we personally seek it.

The work of the Holy Spirit is also to empower us, to control us, to direct our *every* action. He is a person influencing us as we make ourselves available for His influence. Since His direction is perfect, we will achieve the maximum good within our lives as we let Him direct us.

There are positive results of letting the Holy Spirit control our lives: love, joy, peace, patience, kindness, goodness, faithfulness, gentleness, and self-control. Of all life's influences, that of the Holy Spirit will bring the greatest rewards.

Quench Not

I like the verse in 1 Thessalonians 5:19: "Quench not the Spirit." I wonder if we not only quench the Spirit of God from moving in our lives, but also quench the efforts of many who would have a positive impact upon us.

We can stifle or quench the good in others by negative attitudes. On the other hand, we can flame the fires of a positive life with very little effort. A man buoyed me up tonight with a positive word, and it came at a time when I was down, and I had asked God for His special presence. Just a few positive words, shared with no fear of personal rejection, and God's Spirit became more real in my life.

All kinds of attitudes can be quenching forces—anger, fear, depression, a lethargic attitude! All of these must be fought. We can handle this mentally at times, but the only sure way to overcome our quenching God's Spirit within us is to let God's Spirit have control of our lives. The results of God's Spirit residing and controlling our spirits is a new sense of love, joy, and peace.

Church

I've been thinking today about church. What is it? Why does it exist? What is my relationship to it to be? What is a church ultimately to be?

I sense the church to be the sum total of those who have Jesus Christ in their lives. The purpose of the church is simply to share the Good News of Jesus Christ with lost mankind. When struggle or conflict exists in this "sum total of those who have Jesus Christ in their lives," then it's not Jesus living through them but rather a return to our natural selves. Obviously, Christ would not struggle with Himself.

When I let "Christ in me" relate to "Christ in you," there can be nothing but sheer joy. It's a beautiful harmony. The church, then, is only the church of Jesus Christ when there's this kind of love. It follows, then, that our task, as the church, is to let Jesus Christ control our very beings.

Ten Commandments

God's basic law for man was set down in the Ten Commandments. We have embellished them and overlaid them and expanded them, but never have we seen a better description of how man is to react to God, his family, and society. The first four laws talk about what our relationship should be to God; then the next one, to our family; and the remaining five, to our fellow man.

Many cultures have set down similar sets of law, including the Code of Hammurabi established several centuries before God gave the Ten Commandments to Moses for the people of Israel.

You will do well to follow each of the laws of God. For example, "Thou shalt not kill" can be expanded from taking a person's life to murdering his reputation or doing something that would kill his spirit.

Selfishness is the root cause that prompted God to set limits within which we are to live. They're good, and we ought to think about each one on as broad a basis as possible.

Relationships

One of the most real evidences of Christ's presence in our lives is whether we reach out and touch the lives of those around us.

Touch

You've heard the poem "The Touch of the Master's Hand." It's beautiful to sense that our Lord, Jesus Christ, reaches out to us on a constant basis to touch our lives. There's something special about touching another person. It connotes a caring, intimate relationship.

Some of our religious leaders, including the pastor and writer Ralph Neighbor, share how we can become involved in "touch" ministries. This is where we go out to relate to those in need around us. There's a real need for this in our world today where there's a tendency toward the impersonal.

The touch can be physical, but not necessarily so. Expressing love physically, through a warm handshake, a slap on the back, or an embrace is fine and should be encouraged if it's natural. Within the immediate family, it's a necessity for proper growth and maturity.

Reach out to others, share yourself with them and let them share a part of themselves with you. The rewards will be great.

Communication

I've found that one of the biggest problems in life's relationships is caused by lack of effective communication. It's prevalent everywhere; yet there's an answer:

> Love *communicated* will provide the cement that will hold together and build the marriage relationship;
>
> Ideas *communicated* will build a business to the highest level possible;
>
> Empathy *communicated* will generate understanding among all people;
>
> The Good News of Jesus *communicated* and accepted will save man from sin.

Like anything else, effective communication is a learned art. Communication is natural, but it might not be positive. To be effective it requires effort on our part. The key is, we can learn to communicate in a beautiful way in which others are strengthened.

There are some basics: be empathetic; be sensitive; share yourself; never try to hurt someone with words or actions; don't try to be too technical. Remember, everything you are doing and everything you are is communicating; so be sensitive to what you're saying to others.

Reach Out

I believe one of the most real evidences of Christ's presence in our lives is whether we reach out and touch the lives of those around us. Man without the influence of Christ is self-centered and usually self-seeking. Christ reached out to those that came into His sphere of influence. He taught them. He healed them—physically, mentally, and spiritually. Christ did what we should do. He reached out and touched people both figuratively and literally.

I love the song "Reach Out and Touch." It demonstrates good theology. I know when people reach out and touch my life that there's a lift. And I see others influenced as I reach out and relate to them where they are.

Never hesitate to reach out. It can start a chain reaction. You touch the life of a young man; he, his father; the father, his wife; the wife, a friend; and on it goes. You particularly have a lot to share. God has been good to you; so reach out and touch.

Cliques

One of the most devastating social groups is the clique. It's devastating to those kept out because they feel unwanted. It's also devastating to those inside the group because they miss the benefits of relating to a new, fresh person.

The clique isn't isolated to any particular age group. We see it among the very young, teenagers, and adults. Nor does it have a prescribed size. It can be two people who relate only to each other or a group as large as a church that won't allow others in.

Cliques are barrier builders—inbred, selfish, and limited in perspective. Their members close themselves to new ideas or innovation. Whole people don't need the false security of the clique. They remove their "group mask" and become one with whomever moves into their circle.

You should avoid being in a clique where others have no access. Help break down these types of barriers with your peers. You'll be the beneficiary.

Ask

To ask is to transfer the initiative from yourself to someone else. A lot of us don't like this. We like to maintain control ourselves. Yet, in business, I've found it best to *ask* people to do a particular task rather than merely ordering them. People respond better when they're asked.

I feel people everywhere are just waiting to be asked to do something. They don't move off dead center, because no one has asked them.

Asking builds relationships! I sometimes ask someone to do something for me which would be easier to do myself but sharing tasks brings people together. People *want* to do things for others. They just don't know how to take the initiative. Asking, then, is a form of releasing potential.

To ask has other meanings. It's a way of learning from others, but we go unknowing if we don't ask. Again, people like to share what they know; so ask. You will ask some important questions in life: "Honey, will you marry me?" "Hey, can you help me?" "Lord, will You be the guide of my life?" Ask away; it's fun!

Dependent

To some extent we're all dependent on others. While you're young, you're dependent on your family for your well-being and livelihood. Someday it could be just the opposite—we could be dependent on you.

Our society is a dependent society. We're all dependent on each other for various items of specialization. Very few people are completely independent—even for short periods of their lives.

> If I want to accomplish God's purpose in my life—and I do—then I make myself dependent on the power that comes into my life through the Holy Spirit.
> If I want to be an effective part of the Body of Christ—and I do—I make myself dependent on the rest of the Body.

There's nothing wrong in being dependent, within the proper perspective. It only becomes inappropriate when we fail to do our part and make ourselves totally dependent on the work of others. Too many people in our society are doing just that today.

Remember, I'm dependent on you for many things, as I am on many others. You, too, are dependent on me and many others. Sense when it's proper to be dependent and when you need to be independent.

Availability

Today I experienced the joy of being available to God. Sharing at the national lay-renewal conference in Atlanta I discovered again that it's not ability but availability that counts.

I had little idea what to share on the subject "God's *New People* in Business," but God was able to do His thing through me.

Because I was available, I received three invitations to share at evangelism conferences.

Again and again God affirms that He uses those available to be used. It's fantastic! This week I heard Carliss Odum, a cerebral-palsy victim, through whom God communicates so meaningfully. Saved at fifteen, God ignored his handicap and reached down, touched his life, and sent him on a mission to share the majesty of our miracle-performing Christ.

Serving

Today a man asked me, "How much of my effort should I expend serving others?" He then went on to discuss the problem he was having in establishing priorities. I believe the greatest joy in life comes to those involved in serving others. The role of the deacon as described in the Bible is that of servant. The early church set them apart to serve the needs of the group. That's one reason I'm thankful to be a deacon.

Serving is living! It's helping meet people at the point of need in their lives. There's no limit to its application in business, in the home, in our churches—everywhere.

Selfishness has been identified by some theologians as man's basic sin. Other more specific sins grow out of this root cause. As we serve others we are able to overcome this basic nature of man. You'll find, as you grow older, you'll be happiest when you're serving others.

Bonds

What is it that builds bonds among people? Is it love, family ties, common interest, nationality, spiritual values? It is all of these and much more. One of the things I've been conscious of this week has been prayer. I believe praying with someone draws you together as both are drawn closer to God.

This afternoon I met with another member of our church's

long-range planning committee and with one of our associa-
tional workers. It was exciting to experience the bond that grew
among us. When we prayed, God just brought us together beautifully as we jointly prayed for a special insight as to what our
church should be involved in as it relates to special ministries.

Causes also are bond builders. It's important that our causes
are good, and those to whom we bond ourselves are worthy. To
bond means "to fasten"—to bring together to a point at which
you almost become one. It's not casual. It's hard to loosen ourselves once we're bonded together. Therefore, it's a key concern
of life that we bond ourselves together for solid, valid purposes.

Bond yourself to God, to your family, to those who would
edify you, to worthy causes. Let God's Holy Spirit be the bond-
ing agent. He will provide the influence for overall good in your
life.

Divorce

I went to see a man today who was absolutely alone. It was a
sad sight—a one-room apartment, with the door open, inviting
the world in. But no one came until I came to see if he had any
special needs. He told me of his recent divorce and misfortune
in finding a job.

This visit reminded me again of how terrible divorce is. God's
Word says, "And they shall be one. Let no man put asunder what
God has brought together" (*see* Mark 10:8, 9). Obviously, some
divorces are unavoidable, but to live in a culture in which the
divorce rate is skyrocketing is to live where God is not in control.

Marriage is such that we should not enter into it lightly as is
being done today by too many people. They figure that if it
doesn't work out, they can end it quickly. This casual attitude
takes its toll in so many ways—emotional instability of the marriage partners and kids, monetary cost to all parties, social costs,
and on and on the list goes.

While marriage is a long way off for you, consider even now
the partner God wants for you and be praying for her as she's
growing that she'll be and you'll be all God wants from both of
you.

Affirmation

We all need affirmation. Some of us need it more than others. We don't just need it generally; we need affirmation in specific areas of our lives and by specific people. Affirmation by Mom is more important to me than any other person. I can't tell you how important it was for me this past week when you said to me after I shared with the Baptist men's group, "Dad, you did great tonight—better than I've heard you before."

We had a "circle of affirmation" tonight in our lay renewal— members affirming other members. I'm emotionally touched every time I share in such a service. I'm particularly moved when a husband or wife affirms the other or a child affirms a parent. I did notice one thing, though: affirmation is more than just bragging about the abilities of a husband or wife; it's sharing the love relationship with others.

Learn to affirm other people. It helps them and you. Also learn to accept affirmation. Use it to mentally resolve to be a stronger, more effective person.

Praise

Praise is power. It fuels our relationships—no matter if it's God we're giving praise to or whether it's family, friend, or stranger we're praising.

Praise should be real and not done in a self-seeking manner. Don't praise for the benefit it will bring you but, rather, praise with a sense of honesty. It's true, though, that it will strengthen both you and the person receiving the praise.

You should particularly praise those close to you when appropriate. After a special meal or a personal favor, praise your mother. When your sister does something special, recognize it with a little praise. When a friend accomplishes something special, celebrate with them through praise.

Praise to others, especially God, will benefit both you and the recipient of the praise. Even praise little things. They will then be more important.

God's Love

We sing, "It's love—it's love—it's love that makes the world go round." Then we add, "It's you—it's you—it's you that makes the love go round." Love is the cement that binds relationships together. Love binds us to God. Love binds me to Mom, to Val, to you. Love binds the church together.

Without love man is empty—in relation to God, in the marriage and family relationships, and in the Body of Christ. God's Word speaks to us of the need for love: "But the greatest of these is love." In the commandments it's said we should "love *God* with all our hearts, minds and souls," and "love *others* as ourselves." Here, then, we see the pattern for love: God first, others second, ourselves last.

Love generates action. "For God so loved . . . He *gave* . . . ." You know and are assured of my love when it's demonstrated. I can tell a brother, "I care," but if I fail to help him, I have not demonstrated love.

Share love openly and enthusiastically. Love is not taught by rote or programmed, but springs from deep feelings. Obviously, we must have those deep inner feelings through which we learn to really care for others.

Fellowship

Man is not intended to be alone. God made him special—a social being. He established marriage, the family, the church— all to provide us with fellowship. Christian fellowship is beautiful. Today I had lunch with two Christian executives. It was fantastic as we shared together our Christian experiences. Bonds were built that will go beyond casual business acquaintanceships.

I sense God brings us together like this for the joy of the experiences and to strengthen our Christian faith. The best times I've ever had have been in relating to others from a Christian perspective. This happens on a one-to-one basis as well as with groups. God builds ties that go beyond our natural inclinations. I especially sense this since I tend to be reserved, and even isolated, in my own nature. I thank God He changes that.

Sacrifice

We need to learn how to relate to the concept of sacrifice in our lives. Throughout life's experience you will see it demonstrated in many forms:

> the individual making personal sacrifice for the good of
> the group;
> a parent sacrificing for the well-being of the children;
> a friend sacrificing time, money, or energy for one he
> loves;   .
> a community reaching out to those less fortunate.

It happens constantly. We need to relate to it and recognize the need for it in our own lives. We know the ultimate sacrifice was that given by Christ—His life for mine and yours. As a part of Christ's church, we are to give ourselves to each other as needs arise, such as counseling that family in trouble, or giving financial help when there's a material need.

True giving is sacrificial giving. Then we are the ones who gain.

Help

To help someone is man's greatest honor. Our American way is built on the concept taught by Christ. He said, "Do unto others as we would have them do unto us" (*see* Luke 6:31).

Help comes in a number of ways. They are limitless. It ought to become a basic part of our lives. This is one reason I like the United Way. It's an organization through which people help people.

Help can be on the simplest level: an encouraging word, a kind deed, a thoughtful act. Our helpful attitude should reach out in every direction to all people. Help by picking up that piece of trash or by eliminating that wasteful use of energy.

Try to actively learn to help others. You can do this individually and as a member of a group. Later in life your vote will be a means by which you can express your willingness to help. As you help others, you'll be helping yourself.

Kindness

The world today needs a little more kindness—real consideration of the other fellow and his needs, a little lift to the stranger, as well as the friend. It takes so little to be kind—a smile, an attitude. This might be the best thing we can do for a person. I know I relate better to those who have the ability to show kindness.

It's not the easiest thing for a teenager. There's a natural self-consciousness. But, as a matter of fact, most adults still feel the same self-consciousness. But experience tells me it's worth the little effort. The dividends are tremendous.

Kindness should not be a selective thing. It should become a natural part of our lives. Someone told me how much a telephone call meant; another heard of our special prayers when in the hospital. These are little things, but they build bridges of understanding and love.

Since we tend to take those close to us for granted, we must consciously seek to be kind in both deed and attitude with them. God's Word says, "Be ye kind . . ." (Ephesians 4:32).

Compassion

Man's relationship to his fellow man mirrors his inner being. It's one thing to say we care for the needs of others; it's something else to care enough to do something about our deep feelings.

Compassion is feeling for others, but it's more than that. It's feeling tied to action. Just being sorry for the condition of another person isn't real compassion, but it moves in that direction when we start to do something about the situation.

Compassion is related to sympathy and empathy but includes a plan of action. It takes an aggressive spirit and a disciplined mind for most of us to be really compassionate.

Learn to feel with others. Sense their needs. Be aggressive in trying to help. Develop a plan of action. This kind of spirit needs to be developed first in the family—those closest to you. Sense Mom's needs. Reach out to her in love. Really care what's happening in her life. Do the same for others. A warm compassionate heart will bring real balance to your life.

Together

Together! A beautiful word! God intended a togetherness—in the marriage relationship, within the family structure, within society. While we need some time alone, man is a social being. He's at his best when he's working together with others.

Together means the most to me—with you, Valerie, and Mom. There's no one I'd rather be with more. I find more excitement with you, more mental stimulation, more spiritual realization, more fun in every way.

I have found that we get more done together. This is true in business, in the community, in our churches and in our homes.

We recently shared on the idea "I can." It's also important to remember "We can."

To work effectively together requires love. I love you with all my heart, soul, and body—my entire being! So does God! Capture the real essence of life by sharing it together with me, Valerie, Mom, your friends, and, most of all, with God.

Teamwork

As you look at most types of organizations, you quickly see the need for teamwork. Teamwork requires individuals to give up some of their individuality for the sake of the team. In this, both the individual and the team benefit.

An effective team pulls together the best traits of its members to accomplish the maximum good for the group. Of course, you have to be farsighted. The younger team members need to be trained for the long-term benefit of the team.

The church is a good example of a God-ordained team at work. The Bible teaches the need of everyone to use the gifts God has given them and not to worry about the gifts we don't have. School is another type of team effort—different in nature, but still a team. The same is true of the family.

Learn to assert yourself as a team player. Work with those around you. You need them, and they need you.

Retreat

Mom and I have been here at the cabin for two days now. We're having a great time. It's the first time we've been here, just the two of us, since we built the cabin seven years ago. I imagine there'll be more times like these in the future as you and Val have more activities of your own, such as your choir trip this week.

We've had tremendous times here with a variety of people in all kinds of weather. I remember the deep snow, and your and my getting lost because everything looked the same—white. I remember the time with Arthur and Sherry Blessitt, Owen Cooper, former president of the Southern Baptist Convention, and myself, seeking God's direction for Arthur's ministry.

God has been good to us. This is just one of those little evidences. We've had your friends here—Billy Counts, Greg Grice, Mark Reon—and Val's friends—Karen Klemetsrud, Pam Turner, Kim Camp, and Janet Sudak. And, of course, a lot of our friends have enjoyed God's beauty from here.

I hope you never lose contact with the joy of being away at the cabin with Mom, Val, and me, or someday with your own wife and kids. It's a good retreat where we can relax, be close to God, and recommit ourselves to God and His tasks for us in life.

Family

There's no one I'd rather be with than my family. Tonight we had a beautiful dinner together at one of the finest restaurants in town. I enjoyed it tremendously, but more than anything else, I just enjoyed being with you, Valerie, and Mom.

> It was fun to laugh at the time we tried to eat out at this same restaurant and were turned away because we had on sport shirts and tennis shoes.
> It was fun to reminisce about our vacations in Europe.
> It was fun to share about the things that are happening right now in your life and Valerie's.
> It was fun to anticipate the future such as your having your own car in nine months and twenty-eight days.

I guess in all that I do, I get more joy out of just being with you, Val, and Mom. Doing things like pulling weeds, washing dishes, discussing the stock market, sharing mutual views—just being together. I thank God constantly for my family.

Brothers

Today is my brother Richard's birthday. It reminds me of that unique relationship between brothers. What I remember most about my brothers are the pranks they played on me as youngsters. They convinced me the hole under our house could be unplugged and the Chinese on the other side of the world could come through. I remember a lot of fearful dreams about that.

I'm also thankful that I have brothers I can really respect and look up to—all in a very special way. I've enjoyed seeing them grow, just as I have, physically, emotionally, mentally, and most important, spiritually. I'm especially thankful for the rare privilege of having been able to work with my brother, Jimmy, in lay renewal. I've seen what a beautiful character he is, and how he can relate so easily to others. A special love has developed because of this. I only wish I could have my brothers close enough, physically, to have that same relationship regularly.

While you have no brothers, you can be a good brother to Valerie. It will enrich her life, and you can draw on each other's resources.

Sister

You are a lucky guy! You have the best sister any boy could ever have. She loves you more than anyone with the exception of your mother and dad. I have experienced that same love with my sister.

I'm particularly glad that you and Valerie are as close as you are. It's good to have someone you can talk to on a confidential basis without any fear of disclosure of personal things, She has become as much a buddy as any sister can become.

I know you recognize her uniqueness and draw on it. In a similar way, you should be a good brother to her. Help her in every way possible.

As you relate to Valerie, learn how to relate to other young girls. Never treat any girl in any way you wouldn't want your own sister treated.

With a sister, you're building a lifelong relationship. You'll be forever thankful if you build with love and understanding. She will go more than halfway as you're building.

Father

I thank God constantly that He gave me the privilege to be a father. I thank Him that He entrusted the care of both you and Valerie to me and your mother. Being a father demonstrates to me how much God must love me, because I love you so much, and I know God loves us even more.

Like most fathers, I brag about your accomplishments every chance I get. It's because I'm so proud of you. Like God, our heavenly Father, sees and knows our sins and weaknesses, I see and know yours, but it still doesn't affect how much I love you.

As your father I have great dreams for you, but I want you to seek out your own direction under God's leadership. I'm happy just to see you grow tall, strong, well-adjusted, happy, and self-disciplined. These traits can be harnessed by God so you can reach your personal potential.

Always know you can do nothing that will separate you from my love or from the love of God. Also, always know we're both prepared to help you all you'll let us.

Mother

Today is your mother's birthday. It should remind you of the importance of your relationship to her. No person on earth loves you more than your mother, even though it's hard to see how someone could love you more than Valerie or I.

As a young man, it's natural to assert your independence, but age never should free you from the beauty of this close relationship.

Discipline from your mother is sometimes hard to take, but accept it as being good for you. Talk with your mother. Share intimate thoughts with her. The results will be fantastic.

Never underestimate the importance of your relationship to

your mother. Consciously build the relationship. Love your mother and demonstrate it! Work with her! Have fun together! Obey your mother. She would never ask you to do anything that wouldn't be good for you.

Relatives

One thing we can't get away from is the fact of relatives. This can be a real blessing, if we let it be. Or relatives can become worse than could be imagined. I love my relatives and visit them as often as possible. You need to learn to do the same, particularly those closest to you: aunts, uncles, cousins, and grandparents.

Friends may come and go, but your relatives are forever. You need to learn to cultivate them through real friendships. The Bible also gives us instructions for caring for those in our family.

Conflict among relatives is useless. Sometimes it's caused by the division of an estate. Money or material things aren't worth any conflict between relatives. Love, help, and stay close to your relatives.

Valerie

Today is Valerie's birthday. I am proud of the way you demonstrated your love for her by getting her the stereo for her car. It shows again your generosity—the last of the big-time spenders!

I think it's great how you and Valerie get along so well. I'm constantly amazed at the beauty of your relationship. Many others notice it too, for which I'm thankful.

Valerie is special in many ways, just as you are. She has an unusual learning ability, just as you do. She is well liked by her peers, just as you are. She has a special charisma about her, just as you do.

Just as you and Valerie are alike in many ways, each of you

also has a special uniqueness. That's the way God makes us, and it's great.

Thank God for Valerie and care for her. Each day I thank God for each of you and the potential within you.

Friends

The selection of friends is a very important factor in our lives. If we select the right ones, they can bring joys throughout life; the wrong ones can lead us down the path to destruction.

The key friend and comfort, of course, is Jesus Christ Himself. Our family members, also, are not to be excluded from this wonderful circle. From there the world is wide open with people willing to have an impact upon our lives—some good, others bad.

Select friends carefully, judiciously, after much consideration. Establish criteria for selecting. Remember, they play a part in molding your life, as you do theirs. Friends should build each other, be a comfort, a haven.

Work at selecting the right kinds of friends, then be a good friend. Your sister wrote in her article "Joy—the Magic Formula" that real joy in life comes from putting Jesus Christ first, others second, and ourselves last. When we can do this, we know how to be a real friend.

Extra Mile

Because everyone is not willing to adjust or compromise, many times we are called on to go that extra mile. It happens in our home, at school, at church—everywhere.

The key is this: It doesn't hurt to go that extra mile. In fact, there's a little extra joy on that part of the journey—not that we ever go that extra mile to lord over someone else how we're willing to give in, to make the extra effort.

We don't go the extra mile for credit. We do it to accomplish a goal, whatever it might be. When you and Val disagree on whose turn it is to clear or wash the dishes, to solve the problem of neither of your having enough time, I might go that extra mile and do the job for both of you. It solves a problem for both of you and only costs me a little effort. It's much better than your fighting about not having the time.

Be willing to go that extra mile. It will make life easier for others and you. The extra mile is the easiest and shortest mile.

Gratitude

One of the things that seems to be missing in our world today is gratitude. We don't tell people enough that we appreciate them, what they've done, or what they mean to us.

One of the most cherished things I enjoy is a letter from a person sent out of a sense of gratitude. It can be for the simplest thing, but it expresses a feeling that's important.

We should be grateful for what people do for us. If this is so, we ought to show it. These personal expressions of gratitude become real "love letters," and love ought to be given more easily.

If you are grateful for something, learn to express it. It will help you and the person on the receiving end. One of the keys, of course, is that we need to really be grateful. So consider what you have, how you got it, who gave themselves to you, and be very conscious of it. Then, out of a sense of gratitude, share yourself with them.

Debts

At various points in our lives it's natural that we create personal debt. In fact, it would almost be un-American not to borrow money from time to time. But it's very important to be able to keep our debts in perspective to our ability to pay.

Last night a young man called to tell me he was sending a check to pay off a loan I made to him a year ago. I thought that was great because a new need came up last week in which those dollars can be used for God's purposes. But at least three or four others have borrowed money from me in the past, and I've heard no word at all as to their intention to repay. Be sensitive to borrowing money and be sure to meet your commitments to repay what you borrow.

People

I can sing today: "This is the day that the Lord has made . . . ." It's been fantastic! I've heard many share today the truths of the Christian life: Bruce Larson, Ken Medema, Findley Edge—all beautiful people.

I sometimes marvel at the effect people have on me, and I doubt if I'm unique. We learn from each other. Therefore, it makes sense to expose ourselves as often as possible to those people we *want* to influence us. That's the way it's been with the Reid Hardins, the Arthur Blessitts.

I'm going to seek out again an intimate, small sharing group that I can relate to on a more personal basis. The group in Miami taught me many things. I want to continue to experience these types of relationships.

People are also having an impact on you, and you on them. So select carefully those people you're with. All of us definitely should seek to be God's new people.

Race

Today we visited a community day-care center and shared Christmas gifts with the children there. We didn't know before our visit, but all except one child were black. We had great fun sharing and visiting with the children. All kids are fun to be with, but I particularly enjoyed this visit. It reminded me again that there is not enough sharing together as blacks and whites.

I'm thankful that I sense no prejudice in any member of our family. But lack of prejudice in our world today is not enough. It seems to me that on a voluntary basis we need to encourage more mutual involvement. I've enjoyed working with blacks at Florida Memorial College, in Boy Scouts, at the United Way, and many other community organizations. These groups, by the way, have done a better job at sharing together than our churches.

Our ability to work together, share together, worship together—just live together—will determine the peace and harmony of our community, our nation, and even our world.

Relationships

I am made constantly aware of the effect of our many relationships on our lives. Individually, we're given sustenance by our intimate relationships. The strength of our family, and the degree to which we use it to strengthen our lives, is determined by the degree of love and mutual trust developed in the various relationships. The strength and commitment of a community depends on how well relationships are built.

You are at a time in your life when your relationships are all important. Goals should be set and worked at. Intimate relationships take a long time to develop and should be cherished. Don't worry about not developing close friendships yet in your new school or church. Just relax, stay open, and it will happen at the right time. In the meantime build existing relationships with long-standing friends and family. Expose yourself to every opportunity to strengthen old friendships and to make new friends. Remember the total of your relationships—your relationship to God, family, and friends— makes you what you are.

Others

As a young man, you are very aware of yourself. You are self-conscious and introspective. As you continue to grow, learn to consider others. Think about how they feel. Be empathetic. You have within yourself the ability to influence the attitude and behavior of a good number of people—your family as well as friends and acquaintances. Think about it. Let it influence your actions.

We don't live in a vacuum. We are social beings. The sooner we learn to live together in harmony, the sooner we'll release our energies to more productive purposes.

Weave yourself beautifully into life wherever you go. Become a more intricate part of the circles you're in. Be knit together, binding yourself to others. In all of life's relationships, consider the impact your actions will have on others. It will bring you fascinating, positive results.

Mask

Many people—in fact, maybe most of us—wear masks. We're afraid to let people know us as we really are. This is a ridiculous approach. It requires an unusual amount of energy, and most people either see through the mask or would like the real person better.

The key to avoiding this problem is to have a basic respect for yourself. God made us like we are or at least gave us the potential to be what we should. So we need to develop those personal characteristics that we can respect.

Being "maskless" throws off those false inhibitions and lets us relax and enjoy living. Why pretend to be perfect when everyone knows that's impossible! This will free us to the point where we can work on our weaknesses and overcome them.

You are a great guy just like you are. So don't pretend—even with strangers. Just be yourself and all God wants you to become.

Bragging

This morning at breakfast here in California with my business associates I found myself bragging about you. I guess I do this often. While your abilities are important to me, I imagine they're not as important to my friends. I'm sure they're not as interested as I am. Bragging about you reflects on my being too self-centered—too proud of my family's accomplishments.

Bragging about yourself is really obnoxious to people. We really ought to avoid it. If there's to be any bragging, let someone else brag about you. This isn't something you particularly have to learn, because I believe you brag very little—if at all. Maybe the lesson for you is not to brag by being too cocky—too sure of yourself. This also rubs people the wrong way.

It gets down to just being ourselves—natural. We share openly and honestly without being too self-centered, while at the same time not being too closemouthed. Some people even "brag" about their importance by what they wear or with a practiced walk. Try to avoid this kind of nature. People like humble people.

Pastors

God established two offices within the church—that of pastor and deacon. The pastor is to be the undershepherd of Christ to the church. Christ is the Shepherd that brings us to God. The pastor's role is sometimes difficult and should be sought by one under the direction of God.

Today I visited with our former pastor, Dr. R. B. Culbreth. He shared the innermost feelings of his heart. He has a tremendous love for Christ and has a vision of what the church can become under God's direction. The desire of his entire life is to be available to do whatever God wants him to do. I thank God for men like this to lead us.

One thing about which we have to be careful is that we don't put our pastors on pedestals that separate them from their humanness. Our job is to love them, support them, dream with them, and work with them to build Christ's Kingdom on earth.

Unforgettable

Reader's Digest magazine has featured a series of articles written by guest contributors entitled "The Most Unforgettable Character." A lot of men have had a tremendous impact on my life. I've shared with you before who these men are. But the most unforgettable person is not among these. He's the most unique character—I say that with a sense of love—and the most interesting person I've known. This person is Nick Morley, the international-sales representative for General Development Corporation.

Nick is Bulgarian—of Jewish descent. His father worked closely with the king of Bulgaria before World War II. In fact he introduced me to the king in exile. Nick left Bulgaria as a young boy and later served in the underground before Israel gained its independence.

Nick came to America and accepted a job as busboy in a cafeteria, then as a cloth salesman, and then as a real-estate salesman. Here he hit the jackpot, multiplying his sales contracts into a real-estate company worth millions.

With all this, Nick is very human, giving our church a large sum to aid in a mission project and making a substantial gift to a hospital in my honor—thus making me a founder of the hospital. Nick is a tough businessman and a very warm, unforgettable person.

Girls

One of the best things God ever made is girls! I married one of the best that God created, and we have a daughter—and you have a sister—who is one of the sweetest girls in the world.

Aren't we glad that God made both man and woman and He intended, through marriage, that they become one. It's a beautiful thing and a key part of our success in life—learning to live with God's plan for us, especially as it relates to girls and women.

At your age you'll be experiencing new things with girls. You need to determine early in your life how you will relate to them. There are all kinds of girls: lovely, fresh, wholesome, athletic, studious, outgoing. Some are shy and timid, others are boy crazy. Your relationship to them should not vary according to *their* nature but, rather, should be constant. Good men don't develop easy relationships just because there are easy women. All girls are due a high degree of respect, even if they don't ask for it or seek it.

The relationships you develop should be fun and wholesome. They should build both you and the girls that become your friends into better and stronger people. Life's relationships are a serious business. Treat yours that way.

Dating

This week you will have your first date. It's very important, as you approach this Sweetheart Banquet to which you've asked a special girl to go with you, that you have the right attitude. I know you feel that you're pretty well set, but I think we can review several things.

First is your relationship with the girl you date. You're asking a person to share herself with you; so you need to be very considerate of her feelings. The time before a date and the time after are as important as the date itself.

Don't tease her or prove your independence by avoiding her and relating only to other girls. Let the time before and after add to the experience, not detract from it.

Second, while together on the date, remember who you asked out. Don't avoid her and just talk to others. Try to make the date perfect for her. Don't look selfishly at what you want to do.

Also, recognize a *date* is just that—a *time* to share together. It doesn't have to go beyond that. Relax and enjoy being with someone you like. Don't worry about others and their reactions. With your first date, set a sound pattern for those that will come in the future.

Marriage

Marriage is something far away for you; yet it's something that you need to consider in your formative years. The marriage relationship was established by God. It is a holy relationship. It is intended by God to be a lifetime relationship.

Marriage is basic to the family structure, and the family structure is basic to the health of our society. As marriages become sick, families become sick, and our society then becomes sick.

Solid marriage relationships provide a solid platform for the growth of all family members. You are a better person because Mom and I have a solid marriage. Since marriages are intended by God to be permanent, your mom and I have never even considered the possibility of its being ended. I insisted early in our marriage that we would never use the word *divorce* in any conversation, even in a joking way.

Two becoming one! That's marriage. It's giving up my basic selfish nature for a more beautiful life together sealed by God and mutual love.

Anniversary

One of the most important decisions that I've ever made in life was twenty-four years ago today when your mom and I were married. A man's or woman's selection of a mate for life will determine their degree of happiness. We live in a culture today where marriage is taken too lightly, and as a result, we have more broken homes than at any time in history.

On this anniversary it is a good time to think back about the family we established twenty-four years ago. First, I think that we have grown closer to each other in each of the twenty-four years. We are happier and more fulfilled than ever before.

Then, while we've grown close to each other, each of us has developed individually to a point of personal success. Neither of us has tried to smother the other—but to challenge each other's personal potential. And we believe we've allowed both you and Valerie to develop into unique, capable young people, each with your own individuality. Because of this I can thank God for His goodness in providing these twenty-four years of happiness.

Compatible

There's a chemistry that exists between people. When the chemistry is positive and spontaneous, we use the term *compatible*. At times the chemistry is extremely negative and definitely incompatible. All of us sense this in our lives. There are people we immediately like, and if we're honest, those we don't care for too much.

Within the economic scene it's important to learn to be compatible. There can be no such thing as incompatibility with a customer. To be fair and successful requires a high degree of compatibility.

We can improve our compatibility. That is, if we're willing to make some adjustments to accommodate others.

Anyone can get along fine with one with whom he's completely compatible. The real test comes in learning to live with and to be successful with those with whom we're not as compatible.

Our everyday living requires a striving for compatibility to reach maximum happiness and efficiency. Recognize this need within each of us.

Kiss

A kiss is something special! It's not something to be taken lightly. Judas identified Christ with the kiss of a betrayer. A kiss is proper in an intimate relationship, but it's not something to convey casual affection.

The only girl, or woman, I've ever kissed in a serious way is your mother. In fact, as she's shared with you, it was difficult for me to overcome my shyness to even kiss her. Because of our love through the person of Jesus Christ, I have learned to demonstrate brotherly love with an embrace and kiss on the cheek to girls and women I love in the Lord. Even here we must be careful. First, so that it does not become just something to do, thus having no real Christian meaning, and, second, that we're careful that it doesn't go beyond Christian love.

A kiss is the same for a girl or boy. Its purpose is the same. So remember, as you grow older, not to let the intimacy of a kiss hurt you or the girl you're kissing.

Never stop using the kiss of love with those close to you—Mom, Val, me, or other relatives and loved ones. It builds intended intimacy.

Maturing

What one person sees as failure is merely a stepping-stone for us.

Hear

The world speaks to you from every direction—TV, radio, music—sometimes directly and other times indirectly. We also "hear" by what we see. You can tell what I'm saying by how I look!

You need to know to whom to listen and how to evaluate the source of the subject being covered. A scientist may be great on a technical problem but may be naive on a social issue. Be discerning and consider the sources as to the degree of bias.

Don't let just anyone "speak" to you. Your intellectual capacity is limited, so take in only that which will do you good. Sort out the rest and discard it. As God speaks, or His faithful servants speak for Him, listen well! Hearing will then provide direction for life.

Common Sense

You have one of the most important traits needed to be completely successful in life—good common sense. You have developed this personal characteristic more than many adults do in their total lifetime. But this trait is something you must guard jealously. It's not something you can take for granted.

Never become so technical and detail oriented or sophisticated that you lose that basic feel for what's going on around you. Be sensitive to people and situations and their impact on you.

Common sense can help you in almost any personal circumstance. It requires a high degree of evaluation and determination. You learn to sort out all possible solutions to any particular problem and then determine the best one.

Learn to develop your common sense. It will serve you well throughout your life. Technical knowledge is good and becomes magnified when used by a person with just good, simple common sense.

Analytical

A keen mind will help you enjoy life more fully. As you approach specific situations, you will need to analyze the impact they will have on you.

It's important to absorb all you can out of any particular circumstance. You can learn from anything, whether it's good or bad. A quick, analytical mind will store away valuable data for later recall when needed.

Learn from people, situations, books—life's many textbooks. By analyzing the good and bad in your everyday environment, you can then reject or accept random data.

To learn from people, you should try to develop both empathetic and sympathetic feelings toward them. This will help in analyzing what you can learn from them. Your mind is your key analytical tool. Do nothing to it that will jeopardize its usefulness or trustworthiness.

Discernment

Discernment is an attribute you should seek to develop in your life. It's an ability that I feel you already have to a great extent; so use it carefully and let it become a natural part of your life.

The ability to discern facts quickly enables you to move ahead while others are still considering the facts. It's also important as we relate to people. We can sense when we're being conned or when there's sincerity in what a person is telling us. Obviously, we must be very careful here, because we don't want to accuse a person of lack of sincerity. But it will help us to move to the heart of a situation.

God gives some the gift of spiritual discernment. Many have shared that they think I have this gift. While I'm sensitive to people, I'm not absolutely sure about having this gift. Being sensitive and having a good sense of discernment, I can relate effectively to the needs of people. I'm always thankful for the opportunity to help someone in this way. Be sensitive to people—discerning—and use this ability to help them.

Give-and-take

It would be great if in life all we had were absolutes. Or would it? It could be very boring. Science has discovered certain absolutes in the physical world. Life generally has some give-and-take.

You must learn to accept less than perfection from life's involvements. You'll find no perfect people and few circumstances that have every right quality you desire. But we should accept this as okay. Not that you need to be forever compromising, especially in principle. But it's hard to expect others to want to do just what you want.

Learn when to give in and when to remain resolute in your determination. If the choices are equally good or bad, then choose one that reflects a giving spirit.

Compromise is an art of living. A creative give-and-take attitude will help solve problems and minimize tension. It will make people more comfortable, and ultimately you'll win more than you could possibly lose.

Understanding

Many of the problems that exist in our interpersonal relationships are caused by a lack of understanding. We fail to understand either people's words or their actions. On the other hand, when we've developed that understanding attitude, we've overcome the major hurdle to the solution of the problem.

To understand requires effort. It also helps if we have empathy. When we know the background to a particular situation, we can deal with it more effectively.

To understand means more than merely having information

and knowledge. There is inherent in understanding the ability to assimilate, to get to the heart of the matter, to digest quickly all relevant data.

Understanding gives initiative to an exciting life. To "know thyself," to learn to know others, and to discern opportunities will separate you from the mediocrity accepted by too many people. Keep keen the desire for understanding. It will serve you well.

Judge

It seems that on an almost constant basis, we must make judgments. We judge the actions of others. We judge our own actions. We make value judgments without serious deliberation. We should bend over backward when judging others. Today one of our managers wanted to fire an employee because of a judgment made in the heat of an emotional exchange.

Since we do have to make judgments, we ought to learn how to judge and to be absolutely fair. Young people can be fair and objective in their judgments—I see this quality in you—but they can also make quick judgments concerning peers which hurt deeply.

God's Word says, "Judge not." I believe here we are taught that ultimate judgment is in the hands of God. The "judging" we do should be more an evaluative process that leads us to help others, never to condemn them or to sense any superiority over them. Therefore, it's important as we make value judgments to seek God's leadership.

Choosing

We are constantly making choices. You choose how to greet your family in the morning. You choose what clothes to wear. You choose how you're going to relate to the kids at school. You choose how much effort you're going to expend in your studies.

You choose when to say yes to sin or when to say no. Life is made up of these kinds of choices.

It becomes obvious that what you are is because of the choices you make in life. I choose to succeed. I choose to be happy. I choose to follow God's leading. I choose to help my fellow man to the maximum extent possible.

Your granddad was a good tire salesman. He never asked a potential customer if they wanted to buy a set of tires; he asked them to choose from several possibilities. This is what we do. We choose from alternatives. If we don't affirmatively choose, then, in effect, we choose by default. Therefore, if we want to control life's direction, we will aggressively choose what will be best for us. Choosing is fun!

Right

Basic to man is the concept of right. There is within man the need to have right relationships with others. Our Constitution refers to "certain unalienable rights" we individually enjoy.

I have a feeling that there is an ultimate right in any particular situation. This is what we ought to strive for—that ultimate good. Many times it becomes difficult to determine because all decisions aren't between right and wrong but many between right and right. That's when a practical discipline comes into play. Spiritually, we can trust God to lead us in determining what's right.

Man's basic sin is selfishness. It's demonstrated through almost any sin we can name. A proper concept of right will help release you from the sin of selfishness.

Seek a right relationship with God, with your fellow man, and with your family. The rightness will provide a solid platform for you to become all you have the potential to become.

Do right! Seek right for others!

Lying

I heard it said recently that lying is one of the worst sins man commits. At times it's an easy trap to fall into. People lie in words. Businesses lie in their business practices. Organizations lie as they create public images. Any form of lying is bad. It's a form of stealing, because we owe people the truth, and when we're less than truthful, we're stealing something—tangibly or intangibly.

I'm especially thankful for your basic honesty and truthfulness. When you tell me something, I can absolutely count on it. Never lose that trait which you now possess.

You'll see a lot of cheating in life. All are forms of lying. Cheating in school, cheating, or being less than honest, in our relationships with people—these kinds of things limit our effectiveness with others.

In business, people can lie and cheat for a while and seem to get by with it, but it always catches up. I've had to terminate a number of employees who never developed the habit of truthfulness. Always tell the truth, even if it *seems* to hurt; it really won't.

Consistency

One of the greatest virtues in a good employee, especially a salesman, is consistency. It's the characteristic of dependability. We have some salespeople who sell five houses in one week and have a dry spell for a month. Others consistently bring in one or two sales each week. It's almost impossible to plan for corporate growth when sales seesaw up and down.

Consistency is also important in our relationships with people. A child develops severe emotional and psychological problems when the parents can't be counted on to be consistent. If a child "performs" for the parent and receives laughter one time and a spanking another time, he's not sure what to do in the future. When we can be counted on in our dealings with others, we'll have more opportunities for personal growth.

We mature faster in every way when we are consistent in our actions. Spiritual maturity is difficult for the person on a spiritual high one day and totally defeated the next. You are a consistent person. I can count on you. Use this basic consistency to take a step up the ladder to a higher plateau of living.

Trust

In a lot of ways trust is like love—it brings us into warmer and more intimate relationships with others. There are some people I know that I absolutely don't trust. To work with them is a chore. There are others I'd trust with everything I have. It's fun to share with them.

I'm thankful that you are a real person of trust. In all your life I've never had reason to doubt anything you told me. Your trustworthiness has made you special to your friends. While it's now natural for you to be trustworthy, never take it for granted. It's something you continue to merit through a disciplined life.

You also need to take care as to whom and in what you place your trust. Some people don't concentrate their trust in people but in things. Misdirected trust can bring real heartache. I try not to let down a person who has put his trust or faith in me. It hurts my testimony when people can't depend on me.

Never put your total trust in man or yourself. Your ultimate trust needs to be in God. Only He is completely worthy of our trust.

Needs

Today I began listening to a good tape that pinpoints the key reason for success in any particular situation—recognition of need. I won't do a better job for my company unless I see a need to do so. I can't be a better father without sensing a need. I won't enjoy personal renewal unless I first acknowledge my need.

The psalmist cried out to God, "Search me." He recognized a need in his life for God to search out the things in his life that he didn't fully understand. He saw a need he couldn't handle himself.

It's good mental health to admit that we have needs. Only then can we move on to solve our problems. Sometimes pride keeps us from acknowledging that we ever have needs. We improperly assume that the presence of needs in our lives indicates a weakness. This is ridiculous! Everyone has needs, and the happiest people are those willing to admit them. I've seen beautiful relationships form through a person's admitting his needs and then seeking aid from one who could provide help on a very personal basis. Admit your needs and seek a solution to each of them.

Practical

One of the keys to my temperament is that of being practical. Because I believe this so strongly, it influences everything I do. *Practical* typically is in opposition to *theoretical*. I'll buy theory—if I can see where it can be put to use in practical application. Theory for theory's sake I'll leave to the abstract scientist or philosopher.

In business I see the need to get to the basics, to avoid the time-consuming fluff. In religion, I'd rather get right down to the application to life than talk about vague theological concepts. In speeches, I avoid humor for humor's sake or the sharing of abstract ideas. I'd rather share specifics that I've discovered under God's leadership for living our lives to the maximum potential possible.

I see the practical man solving many problems while the theoretical man is considering the best alternatives. Being practical helps you forget the past. There is no purpose in worrying about it. It's gone, and it keeps us from fear of the future. There's enough for us to do today; so the practical man gets on with getting the job done.

Persistence

Today I closed a transaction I've worked on for four months. It's important to my company. The negotiations were tough at times, but I kept insisting on fairness to both sides. I had to be absolutely persistent. I believe the end result accomplished all I had hoped for.

Many things in life require a persistence. You are now working hard at learning to be your best at basketball. Your persistence has already paid off. You're really getting good.

Growth comes from this constant, persistent determination. Lack of growth, on the other hand, comes from an attitude of negative persistence. Again, we become what we want to become and persistently seek after.

Determination

Of all the qualities I see in successful people, the one most consistent is that of determination. It's not just a determination to be successful but rather a determination to get a job done or a determination to utilize personal potential. I can be determined to be financially successful and not make it. The goal is wrong. Instead, if I determine to do my best possible job, then I will achieve solid financial results.

Tonight I talked to a group of college students at the First Baptist Church of Dallas. I was asked the question, "Can I, as a Christian determined to be financially successful, achieve my goal?" I shared that Christ did not promise us financial success even though He did promise us "a full and abundant life." I then shared that our determination must be to give ourselves completely to God, and as He directs us, we are guaranteed success.

You are a determined person, for which I'm thankful. You're

not so self-willed that you won't listen to reason and consider the alternatives. Determination reaches its highest value when it's not centered on the means to get the most accomplished but when it considers our ultimate goals in life.

Faithfulness

Faithfulness is one of the best qualities of man. Being faithful has a much broader connotation than having faith. It speaks of relationship. Over and over again I'm told of broken promises—broken contracts between people. A man's word ought to be solid—something that can be absolutely depended on.

Since our word sets our actions, we need to be careful to whom and to what we commit ourselves. Bonds between people shape our lives; so we should avoid entering into them lightly.

Particularly during the coming years you will develop relationships and determine life standards that will shape your life. Let them be the kind that will deserve your faithfulness. Then life will be more of a joy, more fun, more of a challenge. Avoid giving your allegiance to anything or anyone that won't bring you closer to God.

Patience

The anticipation of a coming event sometimes is better, or worse, than the event itself. Usually when we face something to which we're not looking forward, we find that it's not as bad as we thought. We've wasted a lot of energy over nothing. Patience is harder for the young. I see patience developed in you already, and that's good. Be satisfied with today. Do what you can and don't worry about what you can't control.

Patience is not just being nonchalant about living. Never get to that point. It's rather a keen desire for good in the future and a determination to build toward that good—whatever it takes.

You can further develop your patience as you set specific goals for the future and work toward them.

It's fun to see life unfold as we patiently seek God's will for our lives.

Timeliness

I feel it's important that we develop a sense of timeliness. There's a right time to move forward, a right time to hold back, a right time for contemplation, and a right time for action.

To be timely requires a real sensitivity. This is true in our relationships with people. It's true in the decision-making process. We have seen that it's the vital point when buying and selling stock.

Many times I charge ahead too fast. I've had to learn to slow down, to let the situation develop, not to be premature. At other times, I move too slowly. I have a good idea, but I don't act on it in a timely manner. A good idea or a thoughtful act to another person means nothing unless it's timely.

A sense of timeliness brings order to our lives. What's good at one point has to be weighed heavily at another. What's said in one circumstance will be completely inappropriate in another.

Timeliness is to catch the wave at the crest rather than as it breaks. It's an art that we must master to be successful.

Flexible

There are very few things that are absolute. Learn these and don't deviate from them. However, in most situations our reactions can be flexible. It's how you handle these times that will determine the direction of your life.

Be easygoing, relaxed, about life. This doesn't imply lack of direction, but rather a willingness to move quickly to solve a problem. The fact is, we can't always control our circumstances; so we should learn to have a sense of fulfillment in meeting these times head-on. You can even turn bad situations into positive ones, depending on your approach.

Hear people out. Don't be dogmatic in word or deed. React to them with a sense of openness and acceptance. We are all unique and different. That's as it should be, so approach people with a flexible attitude.

You have an analytical mind. It will help you to evaluate circumstances quickly. Use this to remain flexible and easygoing.

Key

I notice as I write you these notes that I refer many times to "a key thought" or "the key is." Maybe this is how I think—trying to get to the heart of the matter. We do get involved in a lot of superfluous activities and sometimes use paragraphs to say what could be said in sentences.

We do need to "key in" on things—to be specific. I see, in business, people forever beating an issue to death with rhetoric but never solving the problem. The ability to pick key thoughts from books, magazines, speeches will go a long way in your education.

Learn what's important and "zero in" on it. It will keep your mind uncluttered with useless information. Since our minds are limited—although larger than we'll ever use—we need to store valuable data that will be beneficial to us and others.

A key can open many things. It can open a door to exciting situations. You have within yourself the ability to use your keys to provide a stimulating kind of life. Get on with opening those doors of opportunity.

Perspective

Periodically, we need to stand back mentally and look around and gain a new perspective as to what's going on around us.

A lot has happened to us this year. From my position, or perspective, I can see God's hand at work in all of it. He's brought us to a new challenge in a new city where we've met new friends. There's a new peace as I attempt to gain insight into God's view of things.

A keen awareness, or perspective, is also important as we look to the future. It has a lot to do with vision and our ability to focus in on what the future holds for us.

Learn to bring things into perspective. It's the relational aspect of life—learning how to relate to all the forces—that comes into play in your life. Not only is the consequence of learning fun, the process itself is fun. It sharpens you mentally and helps you establish the proper direction for the future.

Second-guessing

It's easy to second-guess a particular situation—not knowing if our action or another's action was proper or not. But usually it is futile—a wasted effort.

We've seen an example of it this week when we wanted to place an order for stock at a specific price, but the broker talked us out of it. As a result, we lost the chance to make a profit. But there's little to be gained by second-guessing the decision. It's done. I know it's best just to learn a lesson from it and move on.

You could second-guess forever: did we select the right home? right church? and on and on. Knowing that we depended on God for His leadership in these matters, it demonstrates lack of faith to question forever a decision. It also is humanly nonproductive. Move forward. Don't second-guess the past.

Move On

Gordon Highfill preached a great sermon today. He entitled it, "We Must Move On." His text was Philippians 3:14, in which Paul tells us he is pressing toward the mark of the high calling of Christ: "I strain to reach the end of the race . . ." (LB). I relate it to God's telling Moses in Exodus 14:15: ". . . Quit praying and get the people moving . . ." (LB).

We do have to move on. There's no standing still. Next year you'll be in high school; in a few years, college. There'll be adjustments as Val goes off to college. Yet it is good and natural; so we find joy in it. Even so, because of the closeness of our family, the adjustment will be tough. Because Val spends a lot of time with Mom, you'll have to help fill that gap to help make the transition as easy as possible.

Not only do individuals and families move on; so, too, do organizations. My company shows good growth; our church is planning and seeking God's will as we plan to move on.

Sometimes we would like to slow it down, but life is progressive, filled with vitality. It leaves behind in frustration those unwilling to move on.

Think Big

Too many times we fail to reach our potentials, because we just don't think big. Some of the best advice I was ever given was by one of the partners in the CPA firm for which I worked when he told me how to approach my job. "Think big," he said. I find this personally rewarding. Too often we're afraid to consider the possibilities of our ultimate achievements.

Learn to think big while you're still young. You have this ability already in many areas of your life. Don't let the small vision of others hold you back.

Last night I shared again with Dr. Landes about his vision for an evangelistic effort for Texas Baptists. He's thinking big! It was exciting to see Arthur Blessitt as he ran for president in the New Hampshire primary. He's thinking big! Mere man can accomplish much when he thinks big.

Success is never specifically quantitative but rather a mixture of various ingredients, generally qualitative. So, thinking big doesn't necessarily promise human riches but rather the promise of a life of joy beyond comparison.

Imagination

Kids have great fun because they're willing to let their imaginations run wild. I love to work with the two- and three-year-olds at church, because they have little inhibition and great imagination.

We tend to control this as we grow older, and as a result, I believe we lose some of the zest for living. Imagination, when properly controlled, can be very beneficial. With most good things it can be taken to extremes, and we then become afraid to face reality.

The most successful people in business are those with imagination. These are the people who will brainstorm with a group to discover the maximum possibilities or will train themselves to use their imaginations when they're the only one considering the alternatives.

A vivid imagination is developed. Some have more natural inclinations toward imaginative minds, but I believe it's a possibility for all of us. I also believe if unexercised, it dies. So continue to develop that imagination. Try to see clear mental pictures of alternatives. It's fun and rewarding.

Believe

To believe is important! Little can be accomplished in life unless we believe.

Believe in ourselves and what we can achieve in life with God's help.

Believe in our fellow man and recognize his unique contributions.

Believe in our country and its resilient ability to spring back to its greatness.

Believe in God and acknowledge the beauty of His plan for our lives.

To believe is to move forward. Lack of belief creates within us a pessimism that thwarts our personal growth. It's said that two of the most beautiful phrases in life are "I can" and "We can." Those who disbelieve say, "No way," or "I can't."

It's also important *what* we believe. If you set up your reasoning this way, there's no way to fail: "If I know God, through Christ, intimately, He will give me wisdom to know what to believe." Also, the Holy Spirit will lead me to know what to believe. I can learn from God and godly people.

Positive

You know how important I think it is to be positive. Being positive helps us get absolutely the most accomplished. I've said before how negativism saps our strength. On the other hand, being positive adds that little plus to our lives that makes the difference between mediocrity and real success.

Being positive is not just getting psyched up. It's rather a way of life—something that becomes a part of you. It's reflected in your walk, in your voice, your demeanor. Someone kindly said that the words of my television commercial come across clearer than those of the professionals. I believe it's because I say the words out of a deep conviction, a strong positive feel for my subject.

You can *learn* to be positive. For some people it's very natural; for others it's a Spirit-given characteristic. So we learn by giving ourselves over to the control of the Holy Spirit and asking for that special positive mental attitude. So the need, then, is to be cleansed of any negative feelings and filled with God Himself and thus gain the positives of life.

Failure

You don't have to look far to find failure. Yet the failure of others is no excuse for us. We can separate ourselves from the syndrome of mediocrity and failure.

Some days—although it's been a long time now—I have that dark cloud of Joe Bltzspfk, the Li'l Abner character, following me wherever I go. But when I ultimately realize the foolishness of it, I pray for the Holy Spirit to take control of my life and remove that black cloud, and without fail, it has happened. One thing, though, I keep claiming Christ's promise *until* it happens.

Failure is defined by us. What one person sees as failure is merely a stepping-stone for others. One bad grade to some is failure. To you, I've sensed, it's just a means to new resolution in the future. I love that attitude!

Failure is an attitude some people get into—a trap that defeats them. Obviously, anything we view as failure relates to the past. Therefore, we can do nothing about it but learn. The future is ahead, and we can decide, in advance, there will be no failure, only learning experiences.

Encouragement

One of the easiest gifts to give is that of encouragement. To encourage is to lift up, to support. It's something we all need, and something each of us should get in the habit of doing with others.

Encouragement helps one get through trying times. Today I had the opportunity to encourage a young minister about the assurance of God's leadership in his life. You could almost see the load lifted from his shoulders.

Not only does encouragement help the other person, to encourage builds us up, because we can see good accomplished. I rob myself of this joy too much by holding back, afraid of the consequences if I don't come through as "real." I feel I'm most encouraging when I'm loose, and only God can do that for me.

Young people, like yourself, are particularly encouraging to adults. So do things and say things that will lift up, support, and encourage the adults you know. It will build bonds of friendships that will last throughout life. Use this gift within you to help others and yourself.

Mistakes

It's natural to make mistakes. Everybody makes them. While I'm writing this, the airline has boarded fourteen more passengers than it has seats on this plane. They're moving off now and are very unhappy. But this is typical. We all make mistakes of one kind or another. The key is what we do about them.

The best thing to do is to quickly admit our mistake and then to solve the problem. Many like to bury their mistakes. Usually this just causes more problems later. I've seen land developers literally bury hundreds of thousands of dollars in engineering mistakes.

It takes a man to benefit by his errors, but he can. Yesterday I heard a man who was sentenced to fifty years in prison. Now on parole, he learned to trust Christ for direction in his life. He shared that there has not been a day since then in which he has not felt an unusual peace.

Face mistakes head-on. Solve the problems they create. It will make you a bigger and stronger person.

Experiences

Life consists of a series of experiences, or events. The way we approach and evaluate these experiences determines the degree of happiness and success we will have in life. Some people never learn to enjoy everyday events. They seek after some elusive experience that will bring happiness.

Learn from your experiences. You've had some interesting ones. Your travel and the people you've met should all become cherished memories. People like Senator Verle Pope, "The Lion of the Florida Senate," and evangelist Arthur Blessitt have given you a broad background.

We can even learn from unfortunate experiences. They can

make us stronger and more determined to avoid making mistakes in the future.

The best experiences will be in the future. Look forward to them and enjoy them. Share them with others. They will then mean more to you.

Overcome

There are a few things in life that can't be overcome. Martin Luther King helped lead a people through a cultural revolution with the cry, "We shall overcome," and to a fantastic extent, it has happened.

The managers of the company, on my first anniversary with Centennial Homes, gave me a plaque that quotes Romans 8:31: ". . . If God be for us, who can be against us?" There's no question that, on a spiritual basis, we can overcome.

> We *can* overcome the fear that keeps us from reaching the heights.
> We *can* overcome all problems that block the path to success.
> We *can* overcome the forces in life that would misdirect our paths.
> We *shall* overcome when we press toward the mark for the prize of the high calling of God in Christ Jesus.

We need this kind of assurance in our lives—the assurance that there's nothing which can't be overcome on the road to personal happiness. We start the process of overcoming by celebrating life now!

Straightforward

Today I discovered again the advantage of being straightforward. I wanted to invite a leading businessman to hear Chuck Colson share about how Christ had changed his life. I thought about many different ways to attempt to get a positive response.

But I felt God wanted me to move straight ahead, so I did and succeeded. He was more than delighted and enjoyed the meeting tremendously.

This demonstrates again that if we feel we ought to do something, we need to be straightforward about it. This means no pussyfooting around the issue but sharing our real convictions.

If you have someone to approach, do it in a straightforward way. The other person will appreciate it. After all, if they want to approach you, they'll probably be very decisive in the way they move. Be alert and sensitive to your task and then decisive in your action. People will appreciate it.

Acceptance

I believe mature persons exhibit a spirit of acceptance. There are some situations we just have to accept. There are some people that we must accept. The wise person learns what he must accept and what he has the power to change.

Some people are forever unhappy because they struggle with this. They don't accept anything, and they fight everything. The well-balanced person accepts life's situations over which they have no control and the ways of people they can't change.

Marriage requires acceptance of a less-than-perfect person — so do other relationships in life.

Acceptance never relieves us from the responsibility to try to improve a situation. It just provides the maturity to relax while we're working at it.

Attitudes

I've noticed that the happiest people in life are those that have developed positive attitudes. They don't let situations develop which create negative feelings. Negativism robs us mentally, emotionally, physically, and spiritually. You can get more done when you're positive. Learn to accept the simplest of tasks with a fresh, positive approach. Never complain! It doesn't help you or the person to whom you're complaining. Fight it. Be strong!

You'll find your attitude is contagious. Positiveness breeds positiveness! Try never to be the creator of a chain of negative feelings. Be positive! You'll like the results.

Matthew 6:22 says: "If your eye is pure, there will be sunshine in your soul" (LB). This is what we need to seek—the refreshing positive attitude that comes from God's direction.

Effort

Let's face it—we don't expend too much effort unless we have to. I'm not speaking of work that might be required of us but rather an effort that involves an intensity. We seek out activities that require as little effort on our part as possible.

First, I think that we ought to follow our natural abilities as much as possible. This fits into our concept of God's giving us unique abilities and gifts. But we can fall into the mental trap of believing that if something requires real effort on our part, then we shouldn't be involved with that particular project.

The discipline of our total being is necessary to expend real effort: mental, emotional, physical, and spiritual. When I know that I should be doing something, but there are reservations, then I must seek the inner strength to move on to get it done, to take the extra effort necessary.

Don't be afraid to make a major effort to get something done. It will be a stepping-stone to the accomplishment of worthy goals.

Work

One of the most important keys to a successful life is that of learning to work. No one ever taught me how to work. It's something that has developed within me over many years. No one ever gave you that strong desire to work at your homework; you have that strong internal desire.

I've shared with you the poster I have on work. It relates the all-encompassing nature of work. Work is necessary for a well-balanced life. Work is healthy—physically and mentally. Work provides its reward, financially, but just as important, as a fulfillment of man's needs.

The work ethic is basic within Christianity. In America we honor the concept of work. Idleness drains man of his vitality. If you're at a point of uncertainty as to the nature of the work in which you're to be involved, explore new possibilities and work out new personal challenges.

Physical work is good for us—almost any kind—and it should never be beyond any of us. It's important at your age that you discover things to work at. It will round out your growth.

Study

One of my favorite verses in the Bible is: "Study to shew thyself approved unto God, a workman that needeth not to be ashamed, rightly dividing the word of truth" (2 Timothy 2:15). These are Paul's words to a young man, Timothy.

You have a great ability to study hard. It's a good personal discipline. Take advantage of this inclination and make the most of it. Study things that will be helpful to you in the future. Use as many sources as possible so that you will be well rounded. Since you're interested in the stock market, learn all you can about it. Try to separate yourself from mediocrity by learning intently.

Sometimes I wish I had gotten in the habit of studying a subject more completely. There's so much more I could enjoy if I had worked a little harder to broaden my horizons through study such as art, music, and science. We miss a lot when we don't expose ourselves to new learning experiences. So study hard and study from a broad perspective. It will provide rich rewards.

Military Service

It was twenty-four years ago today that I joined the army. For three years I served my country, and then in 1954, I was honorably discharged.

Those three years were a very important time in my life. I learned as much in those three years as I have in any other comparable period in my life. I'll forever be thankful for God's leadership in my life during that span.

During those three years I became a man—fully responsible for my actions. I was also married during this period—the most important decision in my life from an earthly standpoint. It was also during this time that I decided to go to college—another of life's important decisions.

The army threw me in with all kinds of people—college graduates, men who had little schooling, farmers—from a diversity of backgrounds. It helped me learn to relate to all kinds of people.

It also helped me build the confidence that I could do anything that anyone else could. The army was good for me, and I enjoyed those years.

Conditioning

We are a people who are constantly being conditioned to generate a desired response. The entire field of advertising and marketing is geared to conditioning the proper response on the part of the public. As a parent, I'll quickly acknowledge that I have such a love for you and Valerie that I want to "condition" you so you'll react properly in various situations and to various stimuli. Therefore, I would have to say that all conditioning is not bad. But while your exposure to your parents is limited, your exposure to conditioning by other forces, especially TV, seems unending.

Obviously, I want you to be your own man, to find your uniqueness and develop for yourself your own life-style. So, while I don't want to overinfluence every decision you make, I do seek a balance to that which I know you're exposed to through society's conditioning influences. A key desire of mine is that you'll be conditioned by God's will for your life.

React

I used to think I'd make a sign for my office: ACT—DON'T JUST REACT. Too many times all we do is react to the forces in our lives. Someone pushes us in one direction and we hurt; then, someone shoves in another direction, and we move.

Obviously we must react. How we react to certain stimuli will determine the degree of success in any situation. When a person shares a need, we can react in any number of ways: with apathy, concern, counsel, heightening the need, or possibly helping to solve it. Since we *will* react, we need to be sensitive to *how* we react.

There are times when we can't wait to react, when we ought to be taking the initiative, taking specific action. Here's where many of us fail—we are afraid to act. Taking an aggressive posture requires more than most of us are willing to give. Yet that's when things begin to happen. It becomes living on the growing edge of life. Act—don't just react.

Motivation

One of the keys to success is motivation. If you see a person properly motivated, then you'll see a person begin to reach toward his potential. Unmotivated people rarely succeed. Business management involves motivating people to achieve the maximum possible.

Motivation comes in many forms. Money is a key motivator. Fear is used by some. A desire for family security is a good self-motivator. Acceptance by peers or others is always a key motivating factor.

We ought to be sensitive to what it is that's motivating us. Most of the motivation in my life comes from within. It's a part of my basic temperament. It relates to getting the job done as quickly as possible and with the best results possible. Others, especially sales people, are motivated by external forces. These include ego gratification, monetary goals, and many others.

Part of our motivation should be spiritual in nature—to achieve the proper stewardship of our lives. I believe the best and most effective motivator is God. He will motivate us to do only what's best for us.

Concern

Concern precedes meaningful action. I'm involved in a lot of projects, but the ones I work hardest for are those for which I feel a real concern. I become involved. I really care.

We live in a world where concern has become callousness to millions of people. Lack of being involved personally frees them from any concern. Of course, we know this is not the American way and definitely not the Christian way.

Concern is something we can develop if we'll let ourselves learn to care for others. In a similar way we can learn to avoid the needs of others by immunizing ourselves from them. Spiritually speaking, we can be sensitive to Christ's leadership and reach out to others, or we can remain in control ourselves and override the leadership of God's Spirit in our lives.

Concern should be stimulus to action. Action will bring beneficial results. These results will be reward enough for our efforts. So, strive to develop a sense of concern for others. Really care for people. It won't be a burden but a blessing.

Competition

In every direction we turn we seem to face competition. It's natural and good. It keeps us on our toes. In school you're competing with your fellow students. On a national basis you're competing for scores on college entrance exams. In basketball you'll be competing with other young men who want to make the team. Everyone won't make it—maybe you'll be one of those—but there's no need to worry about that. Going out and competing should be rewarding in itself.

While in much of life you'll be competing with others, I believe your key competition should be against your own potential and ability. You might not have enough experience to make the school football or basketball team, but you do have the potential to score high from a scholastic standpoint.

Enjoy the thrill of meeting others competitively, even though you won't always win. And seek to do your thing as well as possible. Competition will add zest to your life.

Rejection

Today Dr. Craig in his sermon taught that all of us at one time or another feel a sense of rejection. The Bible teaches that even Jesus was "rejected among men" (*see* 1 Peter 2:4 RSV). We also see it in other great men of God like Arthur Blessitt.

The lesson for us to learn is not to fear rejection, but rather to know the reason for the rejection. Obviously, we should never give up conviction for the sake of acceptance. To be rejected by some people or some groups is a badge of honor. Rejection can be cruel. Learn not to reject others for trivial reasons. I believe one of the traits that will help us most in life is that of acceptance. Rejection hurts others, as well as ourselves. Acceptance builds both.

Learn to evaluate situations quickly! Learn to reject only what's unworthy and personally harmful. Be tolerant of others and tough-minded in your own personal principles.

Opportunity

Tonight I was given the opportunity to share my personal relationship with God, through Christ, with a group of four hundred people. Fifteen of them made new commitments of their lives to Christ. Ten were first-time decisions through which they came to a saving knowledge of Jesus Christ. I'm thankful for the opportunity to share and that God blessed in this beautiful way.

In business when we have a real tough job, we don't look at it as a problem but as just another great opportunity. To grow, people need to prove themselves successful. As we look around us and sensitize ourselves, we become aware of fantastic opportunities. It's accepting the challenge. The more doors we open the greater the sweet taste of success. The more doors we pass by untried, the easier it becomes to rationalize, "I never get a chance to prove myself."

Learn to seize opportunities, and to put them in priority. Then move out and enjoy the fruit of accomplishment. Do this with your friends, family, at school, and mentally and spiritually within yourself. Opportunities are but the doors to real living.

Restrictions

There are limits or restrictions that we must live within. While the courts are striking down many of the social restrictions as to race, nationality, and sex, we still must live within a society that imposes many restrictions.

I believe the best restrictions in my life are self-imposed. No one is forcing them on me. I set them for my own good. Most of them have been set under God's leadership and affect my spiritual worthiness.

The types of restrictions around us will vary with age, local custom, and law. We must fit into these situations if we are to be happy. This relates to what we've discussed earlier—discipline—especially self-discipline.

Be careful that when in a position to do so, you do not impose restrictions on others that are unfair or that you would not want imposed on yourself. We must maintain maximum personal freedoms and at the same time accept certain restrictions as being best for our total society.

Small Things

Life is generally made up of the small things. There are very few explosive, fantastic events that affect us on a day-to-day basis. Yet these small things have such a tremendous impact on us.

We found out this week that a small leak—just about thirty drops per minute—had done about five hundred dollars' damage to our cabin. A small leak—but a lot of damage. That's illustrative of life—the small things affect the direction of life itself.

Never consider anything you do unimportant. Everything you do has an impact on you and others. I sometimes tell prisoners, "Don't worry about the big things. Learn to do the small things well." I believe this is more a key to the happy successful life than most of us realize.

Don't wait for the horns to blow. Be in there pitching in everything you do. We've known people waiting for that big deal to pop who have missed out on the excitement of everyday life.

See

The ability we have to see is one of the best gifts God has given man. But I wonder if we make maximum use of this ability. Do we train ourselves to see or do we just accept it as a fact and therefore remain casual about it?

I believe we can gain a fuller enjoyment of life by learning how to "see." The blind person does this. He can sometimes see more in a particular situation than we can with perfect vision. It requires an intuitive sense of observation as to what's going on around us. Or, we learn to see through the obvious to the reality of a situation.

As we learn to see, we learn the needs around us. I've always said I support the United Way effort because I can't possibly relate to all the social needs I see all around me in my community. But just as I see, I could also train my mind to block these needs from my vision and remain aloof from them.

To see is also such a pleasure. The beauty of God's creation can't be beat. Learn to "see" the beauty all around you:

> In the attractiveness and inner beauty of that special young girl.
> In the way God brings people together for fun and fellowship.
> In the graciousness that exists in your home because of who's there.
> In the beauty of a meal prepared by a mother who loves you.
> In the everyday glory of living out the life God has given you.

To "see" is a privilege that many miss. Acquire the trait of seeing and enjoying all of God's beautiful creation everywhere you go and all the time.

Feelings

Man is an emotional creation of God. He has all kinds of feelings. How we feel about people, situations, and things affects our life-styles. The control of our feelings determines to a great extent our degree of happiness. I've tried in my life to not let my feelings overpower me. I accept them for fact. There's no denying them, but at the same time, I know I need to control them, not to let them control me.

Some people attempt to smother their feelings. This is unhealthy. It's better to recognize them, even take advantage of them, to strengthen ourselves. When I feel exceptionally good, it's natural to sing. But when I'm down, it's not natural; yet when I let God's power be released in and through me, I can sing in spite of my natural feelings. In fact, my feelings change for the positive.

Accept your differing feelings. Don't deny them or smother them. Don't give in to those feelings that would lead you into sin, but, rather, through self-discipline and God's help, channel your natural feelings into a positive force in your life.

Guilt

Guilt has caused many people to fail to become all they could become. I shared with one person who had carried guilt for over twenty years, and the burden in her life was fantastic. To be her beautiful, fulfilled self, it was essential that guilt be removed from her life. Recognizing it as sin, we prayed that God would cleanse her of that sin in her life.

I know that as a teenager you have feelings of guilt. They must be dealt with and have to be removed from your life. Just as any other sin, guilt needs to be confessed to God, and then you can thank God that it's gone. Never resurrect it in your life. If you confess it, it's gone. First John 1:9 says: "If we confess our sins, he is faithful and just to forgive us our sins, and to cleanse us from all unrighteousness."

Watch out for those things that cause guilt. Try to avoid them. Take the initiative and solve the problem in a positive way. Those sins that are repeated, keep confessing and asking God's forgiveness. Just as I'll forgive you for anything you ever do wrong, so will God even more so. So, then thank Him that He's released you of your sin and guilt.

Limitations

I hate to acknowledge it, but I have my limitations, just as every one of us does. Sometimes I feel like I can do just about anything anyone asks me to do. But when I'm honest about the proper stewardship of my life, I have to admit there are some avenues of service that I need to refuse. My limitations are definitely physical and financial, and probably emotional, as well as many, many other kinds of limitations.

It's important to acknowledge our limitations because then we can get on with doing what we're qualified to do and seeking help in those areas where we need it. Even God has His limitations! Obviously, they're self-imposed, but God limited Himself in His relationship to man. He's given man a free will to choose to follow Him or to follow his own direction.

Once we've admitted our limitations, we're then free to work at building up the positive aspects of our lives, fitting ourselves in where we can reach our personal potentials and helping the organizations we're involved in to reach their potentials. This keeps us from becoming involved in wasteful, time-consuming activities with no clear results.

Becoming

All of us are in the process of becoming. I enjoyed the book *The Becomers* by Keith Miller. It's very evident as we look around us that the way people are is the result of the various influences on their lives and the very private decisions they make.

It's important to strive to be satisfied with what we're becoming. If not, then we need to decide that we want to change and take the positive steps that will lead to a new direction.

One of the women in the church told me that our study and discussion on personal potential and my personal testimony had made a tremendous impact on her husband. She said she wished that they had been exposed to people and concepts like this earlier in their marriage. She sensed her husband "becoming" a new kind of man—more committed to God and His will.

You are becoming; so become all you can be. Examine your alternatives carefully and become all that you can be, using all of God's available resources.

Mental Health

The importance of good, solid mental health can't be emphasized enough in your maturing years. I was reminded again today that many people live a hell-on-earth kind of existence. Life is not intended to be like that. It should be a challenge that requires personal courage, and we should be fulfilled, happy people.

I like the quote: by Reinhold Niebuhr: "God, grant me the serenity to accept things I cannot change, courage to change things I can, and wisdom to know the difference." What we can't control, we ought to learn to adjust ourselves to. What we can change for good, we ought to get on with.

Mental health should have nothing to do with the presence or absence of financial resources. It, rather, has to do with the basic resources available to all mankind—an adequate self-image and self-worth, a sense of personal accomplishment, of even the smallest task.

Some experts tell us that mental-related problems require the use of over one-half of our hospital beds. I realize it's easy to talk of good mental health but not as easy to achieve it. It seems to me the key is the absolute certainty of God's presence in your life and the resulting peace that comes through His control of all we do.

Social Drinking

One of the most wasteful things in the world today is what we term *social drinking*. Drinking is drinking! There's nothing social about it. The lack of drinking has never caused me to be less sociable than one who does drink. And I've never seen a single person become more socially acceptable when he was drinking. In fact, I've seen just the opposite.

Drinking is costly. It cost the life of a relative. It cost the marriage of a friend. It cost the job of a business associate who earned over $150,000 annually. It causes broken homes, broken men, women, and children, broken businesses, and many, many broken dreams.

There's no reason for it. There is no gain—absolutely none. It can't add one thing to our lives—only take away. Since I made this determination early in life, it has never been the least bit appealing to me. All we have to do is to make the decision before the situation even occurs. I'd urge you to make that decision now. It will be one of the best you'll ever make.

Fear

One of the emotions that strangles human initiative is fear. There's no question that fear robs us of meeting our personal potentials. I believe the statement I heard recently—most of the things we fear never happen; so our fear is of no value.

A key cause of fear is not knowing the consequences of future actions. We want to avoid the results of everyday human experiences. This is ridiculous, since it's through trial and error that we learn. We don't even need to fear failure. To fail at times is natural. We have such a winning-oriented society that we never learn how to lose. Yet losing can be as rewarding as winning.

My temperament leads me in positive directions. The fear of

failure never enters my mind, because even if others see human failure, I can point to a learning process. Overcoming fear, or never letting it gain a hand in your life, will put you in a position to lead a positive, aggressive life.

Courage

The attribute of courage is something for which a young man should particularly strive. It will provide the "staying power" in all areas of life: school, family, church, and all relationships with others.

Courage helps us to do things we might think impossible. Courage stirs up the adrenaline within us to accomplish almost any task. Courage provides its own reward—a sense of personal satisfaction. Courage requires commitment. This kind of commitment is more than "an awareness of"; it's a definite act on our part. Real courage involves action.

I'd like to see this characteristic being developed more effectively in your life. It will give you a personal sense of joy.

Satan

While we don't think a lot about Satan, we see the results of his effort constantly. Broken lives, divided homes, unfulfilled people, inconsistent living—all these and more are the work of Satan.

Today, at the pastor-deacon retreat in Miami I shared what I learned just last week from Jesse McElreath—Satan is working to persuade us that we don't need to be involved with prayer, Bible study, a spiritual journey, or witnessing and sharing. And if Satan isn't successful in persuading us, then he'll pervert these activities within us. We'll become so single-minded or heavenly minded that we're no earthly good.

Satan is real—just as sin is real. For one thing, God's Word teaches this. But just as important to me, I've felt the power of

Satan and sin in my life when I wasn't depending totally on the
power of God.

Don't be fooled into thinking you can beat down Satan in your
own power. When I'm under a satanic attack, I merely continue
to call for strength through the power of the name of Jesus.
Jesus Christ is victorious over Satan.

Temptation

Temptation comes from many directions. It hits us at our
point of weakness. For me to be offered an alcoholic drink is not
a temptation. In fact, it never has been, because I made a decision as a teenager that I'd never take a drink, and once that
decision was made, it became fact. For me temptation just takes a
different form. Perhaps Satan works on my pride or my determination to get a job done.

You will be tempted. That is a fact. It will tend to be in these
areas: sex, ambition, pride, selfishness, and so on. With age, the
nature of the temptation will vary. The consequences of yielding
is separation from God.

Since God provided the means in Christ to heal the breach
between God and man, the separation is temporary, until we ask
forgiveness. God's Word promises cleansing of all the consequences of sin, so we are then again holy and pure. While temptation is inevitable, as is some yielding, the consequences can be
short-lived.

Maturity

Maturity has nothing to do with age. Some people mature
early, while others never mature. The maturing process is the
process of becoming what we have the potential of being. True
maturity is being well rounded—every area of our lives is in
balance.

One aspect of maturity is the ability to handle our feelings. Our innermost feelings change with age, but no matter the nature of these feelings, a key to happiness is to learn to keep them under control. In effect, they control us, or we control them. The mature person learns to prevent the overheating of his emotions.

Real maturity is learning to accept those things we can't change and learning to change those things that will add to our wholeness as individuals. It involves acceptance of our circumstances. If we lose that chance for a killing on an investment, we accept it and go on. That requires real maturity. If we learn through this kind of experience, that in itself becomes a part of the maturing process.

Measure

Last week I met Gene Getz who wrote the books *Measure of a Man* and *Measure of a Church*. In the second book he describes the key ways to measure the maturity of a church, to determine how it relates to the concepts of faith, hope, and love. Maybe we can relate the idea of measuring up as a young man to the same yardsticks.

To a large degree your personal maturity is measured by the degree of your faith:

> your faith in yourself and your future;
>> your faith in your fellowman and your willingness to
>> work with him;
>> your faith in God and His will for your life.

We have hope because we have Christ within us. Colossians 1:27 says: ". . . *Christ in your hearts is your only hope of glory*" (LB). So our hope goes way beyond man's human limitations. Our hope is because of Christ, not ourselves. The degree of this kind of hope within you is a measure of your maturity.

Then, the most important measure is love. Even simply on an

earthly basis, people measure our maturity by how much we care for others—really care. Love fulfills us. It strengthens us for the tasks of life. Narrow, unhappy people never learn to express love. Love opens our lives to fantastic experiences.

Vanity

Sometimes we get carried away with ourselves. At these times we need to mentally puncture our vanity and return to reality. We can be vain about our appearance, our intellectual ability, or even about our sense of humbleness. Pride is good, up to a point, but when taken to excess, it becomes vanity.

You are a fine-looking young man. You look good in your clothes. But don't get too carried away with it. That's not the real you, or at least it's not the *important* you.

Today we were buying a coat for Mom. We tried to get one that looked good, one that could be worn with most anything, and one that wasn't too pretentious. This is how we ought to approach our appearance—we should want to look neat; our clothes should be practical and not too elaborate.

People like others who are down to earth. They can relate to them more effectively. On the other hand, vain people are very hard to get close to and are usually isolated from the mainstream of life. Avoid being conspicuous for vain purposes. If conspicuous, let it be for the good of others.

Charisma

The quality of charm and grace in a person creates a charisma about him. You need to develop this characteristic so that you'll have qualities within you that cause people to want to be with you and to be drawn to you.

This comes from an inner glow. You've met people you just enjoy being with. Develop the traits you see in them—men like

Arthur Blessitt who have a caring attitude about others and all kinds of people.

Overcome the desire to withdraw completely from others. Relax with people and relate to them. Take their feelings into consideration. As you do this, you can then influence them for good. This will aid you in the stewardship of your life in Christ. Let Him give you this beautiful attribute of charisma.

Aggressive

Some of the most exciting people in the world seem to be those who approach life aggressively. They're not satisfied to just get by or to keep the status quo. I enjoy life most when I move out in an aggressive manner, wanting to accomplish something. In a similar way, when I hold back and do not face the situation head-on, I'm the most disappointed.

The aggressiveness I'm suggesting is not being overbearing, pushy, or selfish, but it has a positive, happy feel to it. It gets things done *for* people, not *to* people.

The Bible says: "If we're neither hot nor cold, God will spew us out of his mouth" (*see* Revelation 3:16). That's what I mean—a warmness about us, an intensity, a vitality.

Because of your natural temperament and age, you need to work on this. I can verify that you seem the happiest when you're aggressively seeking something. Keep it up!

Boldness

In the Book of Acts the early Christians were described as having a boldness. I like that. They were bold in preaching what they believed—the Good News of Christ.

I believe we're to have that boldness in our Christian witness, but I believe it should be more than that. I think it's great when we approach all of life with a boldness. We are fearless as to what the world can throw at us. There's nothing we can't handle.

Boldness comes from strong belief in yourself and the direction you're taking. You can afford to be bold when you're doing what God wants you to do.

So be bold and aggressive in a positive way—never overpowering or conceited. Approach people and situations with an unusual confidence and boldness. It adds to the joy of life.

Pride

There's a tremendous danger in excessive pride. It's self-centered and basically selfish in nature. We need to avoid this and even fight it in our lives. A sense of humbleness and vulnerability to others puts us in a position in which we can relate to others more effectively.

Obviously a sense of personal pride is good but extremes need to be avoided. We should be proud of our country, family, friends, and even ourselves but never to a point of being overbearing and boastful.

The mental and emotional release we attain when we are just ourselves makes us better people to be around. We have to be careful not to use pride as a security blanket of self-protection. An overactive amount of pride indicates a lack of concern or friendliness to others.

Try to balance a proper level of self-assurance and sense of humbleness in your life. You'll benefit fantastically.

Humility

The quality of humility in a person can be one of the strongest forces in his life affecting his relationships with people. It is a quality that can be learned to a point that it becomes natural.

Humility starts within us—a desire that we have to recognize our inadequacies and to acknowledge them to ourselves. It ultimately affects how we relate to others. We've said that man basically is selfish and that selfishness produces all kinds of sins, including pride. This sin must be acknowedged and conquered if we are to have the God-given quality of humility.

I'm speaking of real humility not just pretended humbleness. This false humility in itself demonstrates a high degree of pride. Real humility grows out of love. It congratulates and celebrates the successes of others. This is hard for us to do in our very competitive society.

Humility sometimes is hard for intelligent, successful persons. They need to be reminded of what they don't know and what they can't do—not by others but, rather, through their own self-discipline. You can't control what others think, but more people will think well of you if you develop the trait of humility in your life.

Youth

One's youth is so important to his entire life. It's obviously a time of preparation for the future which we hear emphasized quite a bit. But just as important is that it's a wonderful time in itself. The teenage years represent about 10 percent of your total span on earth. It should be a time that is used effectively, a time that is fully enjoyed, a time when you build a solid foundation for the future.

Many people always seem to be looking to the future for personal fulfillment. God's Word says: "This is the day which the Lord has made; let us rejoice and be glad in it" (Psalms 118:24 RSV). This verse is appropriate for your youthful days. You should and can rejoice in each day. Never wait to enjoy—*enjoy now!*

You are planting seeds in your life that will also be harvested in the future. So see that they are of good quality, properly watered and nurtured. Then not only will you enjoy today, but you'll be establishing the certainty of a fruitful future.

Anticipation

I remember the anticipation I felt as a child on Christmas Eve. There was an excitement that is hard to express. As I grew older, and as you do, the anticipation is not felt as much. Then our anticipation is transferred to other events. My anticipation now ties in to events in your and Valerie's lives such as how you will do in the county spelling bee and how Valerie will do when quoting the first chapter of James in the worship service.

I hope you don't stifle that sense of anticipation, because it adds to the zest of living. I also hope you're anticipating a good ski trip that begins tomorrow. I've found that half the fun of a trip is the planning and anticipation.

Anticipation is similar to discernment. You learn to sense what's going to happen in a particular situation. I'm always trying to anticipate future events. It helps me to lay an effective plan of action. Open up your mind to the future. Consider the tremendous joy that lies ahead.

Different

Sometimes it is good to be different. There's no need to agree with the crowd, if the crowd is wrong. Some seek to be different just to stand out from the group, in effect they are on exhibit.

The time to be different is when you can lead others in a positive direction. The concept that we "dare to be different" is a challenge for a young man your age. It lets you know conformity is not your only alternative.

Accept your difference and use it to maximize your personal satisfaction. Compromise of personal integrity to conform never brings real happiness. Happy, successful people are willing to be different.

Copying

There's a lot of copying going on today. Businesses have become giants because of the need to provide copies easily. There are all kinds of copies—some good, and some just plain phonies.

Mr. Kellstadt, who was the president of Sears, Roebuck and Co., used to warn me about copying the business practices of others. You never know if you might not be just copying their mistakes.

I received a letter this week in which the writer said he tried to copy the deeds of Christ in serving others only to find that the outward action didn't produce the inner wholeness that was so obvious in Christ. The point is, we don't have to copy anyone—even Christ, although the perfect example—but rather simply to let Christ Himself live through our lives. Then there's no problem of the copying process and others see the original. Beautiful!

Learn to be happy with yourself! Don't copy others. Develop the *original* you! Nothing then will be lost in transmission. You'll come through with a good, strong picture of the real you.

Leadership

One of the characteristics that we need to develop in life is leadership. If we are to be successful in any field, we must learn to be leaders.

Not that we should seek leadership roles in every activity. This is a danger. A good leader must also learn to be a follower. In this way he will learn how to react to those providing leadership. In fact, supportive roles can be just as fulfilling as being the leader.

Leadership requires a sensitivity to those being led and that which you want to accomplish through them.

A good leader has these qualities: vitality, endurance, decisiveness, persuasiveness, responsibility, and intellectual capacity. You have these traits now and you should consciously work to improve them. To be an effective leader, it becomes very important that you develop the characteristic of cooperation in yourself and in those you lead.

Minister

You are a minister! I am a minister! Every Christian is a minister! We can then quickly ask the question, "How effective am I in my ministry?" I shared with our church committee on long-range planning that one of the key jobs of the church was to help each of us as ministers to find our ministry.

There are several ways to look at the word *minister*—a minister, to minister, or a ministry. All of these are action words. They get us moving, and that's what life is all about—doing what we sense God wants us to be doing.

Our ministries are as different and varied as we are. I can't do yours, and you can't accomplish mine. It's beautiful to see groups where each person is doing his part. You see it in families, in churches, and, as a matter of fact, in any group of people.

Accept your role—whatever it is. That makes life complete. Do the little things as well as taking on those big jobs. Your effective ministry will aid others in their ministries.

Humor

Life should be fun and happy. Humor will help accomplish this. You have a good sense of humor. I enjoy seeing you laugh. It's great. While I've never learned to tell jokes, I do enjoy good humorous situations. I believe the best are those taken from life. Don't be afraid to laugh at yourself. Sometimes we just have to acknowledge that what we did was funny, or stupid, and laugh it off. It will help relieve the tension at those times.

Developing that keen sense of humor helps us as we relate to others. The lack of humor makes people wonder about us or even fear being with us.

I believe you have an unusual gift in this area; so learn to use it. It creates a contagious feeling of goodwill. We need more of that. It will also help keep that smile showing. That's important, too.

Warmth

To satisfy man's need for warmth, he uses both clothing and shelter. The need for warmth is instinctive. The baby is content when it secures the warmth from the body of the mother. The child feels secure when he knows the warmth that is available to him in the intimate family relationship. As Valerie says, "Give a warm cuddly and not a cold prickly." This indicates the desire of all people for warmth.

I wish I were a warmer person. It's not a part of my basic temperament. Yet I know God can change me and provide a warmth that will give comfort to others and a fulfillment within me. I've seen God do that.

While you're young, strive to provide warmth for others, like Uncle Jimmy does. I believe down deep you have the same traits. All you need to do is develop them. You'll be helping others and yourself.

Warmth is expressed in many ways. Relax and let the warmth flow from you.

Tension

One of the biggest problems with people today is the fact of tension in their lives. On a human level it's difficult to keep from suffering this universal malady. Today, it hit me. The severe pain in my neck is partially physical, but largely due to the fact that I've got tremendous responsibilities this week.

I know how to relieve myself of this pressure; yet there's a discipline involved that doesn't come easy. I know that first I must just give myself over to God and let His Holy Spirit have complete control of my life. After all, I can't do much in my own strength, but with His help, I can do all He wants me to do. This will help me to relax mentally—thus opening the channel for better activity.

People of all ages get tensed up. It's defeating; so it has to be overcome. God will help us. Mental and emotional discipline will also help. Tension can be minimized under these circumstances.

Anger

Anger is one of those emotions that robs us of our happiness and sense of well-being. Almost anything can trigger it: a sharp word, a questioning attitude, being late, or just that we decide we want to be angry.

It just doesn't make sense to be angry. Unless we learn to control it, anger becomes a habit. Even when we have learned a degree of self-control, anger still flares up. It's at these times that we must concentrate on its uselessness and then overcome it quickly.

Long-term anger or resentment can eat away at our health. We must fight it like anything else that would attack us. An evenness of temperament will provide real strength for our lives.

The ability to control any personal hostility will be a testimony to others of the peace that Christ can bring to our lives.

Don't let quick hostility or a sense of wrong toward others or situations rob you of God's perfect peace.

Gifts

God's Word teaches that from those to whom much is given, much is required.

Keepsakes

I love to go back over special keepsakes I've saved from the past. They help me relive the excitement felt at the time. While it's unhealthy to get carried away about the past, it's also natural to reminisce. This is why I save matchbooks from restaurants I've eaten in and save old army clothes and letters received as a teenager.

Your keepsakes will become more and more important to you in the future: your knife collection, the summary of your stock activity, the letters you've received from girls—even though you've only met them once.

I treasure several old keepsakes that remind me of my grandmother, my schoolteachers, and my immediate family and friends. Mom still has the one-dollar bill I gave her to pay for the hayride ticket on our first date—in 1948!

Particularly save those items you love such as an old jacket, a favorite tie, or something that you've carried in your pocket. These keepsakes will help you have a healthy view of the past.

Possessions

Some people will do almost anything to possess what they desire. They seem to feel that possessions will satisfy. Experience has taught me that tangible possessions, while giving a degree of satisfaction, can never in themselves bring real happiness. Since this is true, the giving of material possessions will not build beautiful relationships.

Man is happiest when he's satisfied with what he has. This means not content with the status quo but not insatiably desirous of possessions either. In business I've seen again and again how possessions added little to man's happiness. The desire to succeed is good; strong motivation for success is good, but neither is good when done solely for what a person might possess.

The most valuable possessions are intangible: to possess another's love! to earn and possess the respect of those close to us! to possess a vision and dream of what we can become! All these are tremendously more important than material possessions. Just as material possessions can be stolen from us; so too can these intangibles—love, respect, vision. Guard them closer than you would your financial resources.

Reputation

Your character is defined as the kind of person you really are while your reputation is what people think you are. Both are important—your character being the most important, no doubt; yet your reputation affects your effectiveness in having a positive impact on those within your environment.

You need to guard your reputation. It will affect your success in school, later in your career, in your relationships with girls, and ultimately in marriage.

> If you have a reputation for taking advantage of others, they'll reciprocate with you.
> If you have a reputation of being fair, people will tend to be fair with you.
> If you develop a reputation of being open and honest, it'll surprise you—the openness of others.

Reputations are obviously the result of what people think, feel, and say about you. Through your sincere, not faked, actions, encourage people to think well of you, to feel good with you, and to say only what is positive about you. Ultimately your reputation, though important, isn't the most important thing in your life. It is, rather, what you really are in God's eye not man's.

Character

Your character is you! We've referred to this several times as we've looked at subjects such as testimony, transformed temperament, and reputation. All of these are outward expressions of the real you or, in the case of temperament, a natural tendency.

A person's character is built and shaped. Obviously, it's affected by your environment but not controlled by it. The controlling force is within your own being—your soul and your mind. Evidence of the fact of character's being built is in the phrase we use—"character-building traits." Seeking to develop such traits in our lives will shape and determine our characters.

The highest compliment you can receive from a friend is that you are "a man of character." That, in effect, is what the *Miami Herald* article about me meant when I was called "a man of God." As a Christian my character should be more and more like that of Christ's. After all, like Paul we can say, "I myself no longer live, but Christ lives in me" (*see* Galatians 2:20). As we approach this maturity in Christ, our characters will be all they should be.

Your Name

Robert Bryan Roach. Robert B. Roach. Bobby Roach. Bob Roach. All great names! Today I met a man who considers a man's name important—Trammell Crow. When I met him, he said my name at least four times. There seemed to be a ring to it.

You were given a special name—Robert. You were given the name of your grandfather. This name was given to you, because your mother and I knew no other person whom we loved more or whom we would like you to emulate.

So let your name be important to you and to your parents, family, and friends! Let people say "Bob Roach" with a real sense of respect.

Live up to your name. Create within yourself a person that

others should know. I love to see people's reactions when I mention the names of different people. Develop that reputation and name that people relate to warmly and with love.

Appearance

Your personal appearance is very important to your total well-being. As you become more and more conscious of your appearance, you will note the impact it has on people around you.

I believe the key is appropriateness—not so much what you wear, but if it is proper for a particular situation. Of course, no matter what we wear, we can be neat. Cleanliness and neatness in young people are important because they affect other youths as well as adults.

Obviously, clothes don't make a man. What he is, is what really counts. So don't become overly concerned with what you wear. It seems the proper thing is to avoid extremes in what you wear and in your attitude about your appearance. This relates to your personal grooming as well as your clothes. To make a good first impression, do your best to appear properly dressed.

Time

There's one thing in life that we all have in equal amounts—time. The way we use our time influences our accomplishments in life. Time's not like money. We can't store it up. It's here and then gone. So it becomes imperative that we use it effectively.

Life is exciting when time is used to accomplish specific goals in our family life, at school, and in the community.

One of the saddest things to hear someone say is, "I thought about, even planned it, but I didn't get it done." Intentions are good; planning is good, but they only become meaningful when we take the time to execute them.

Learn to use time. Be a time-saver, not a time waster. Read.

Study. Learn. Travel. Relax. Contemplate. Establish goals. All are good uses of time. By establishing routines that use time properly, you are building for the future.

Voice

You can use your voice to accomplish much good or as a tool that hurts deeply. The voice is a reflection of the real you. I read this past week that a particular blind man can tell if a person is lying just by listening to him speak. Of course, some lie detectors can do the same.

Your voice can be an instrument to give lift to others. I know that others, as well as myself, take great pleasure in hearing you share from a sense of excitement. In the same way, your voice can be used to create negative vibrations within those to whom you relate.

I can hear some voices and immediately feel good, while others have a depressing effect. It's not just the sound, but rather what the sound reflects from the inner being.

Be careful to consider the effect your voice is having on others. It's a part of the stewardship of your life. Let it be used totally for good. In what you say and how you say it, express warmth.

Words

It's hard to overestimate the power of words. What we say or write mirrors what we are. Words can be beautiful or they can be destructive.

It's important that you learn:

to control your words so that they will harm no one;
to use your words to build bridges of understanding;
to use your words to express love to those close to you;
to speak well so that you can express your thoughts clearly.

You have an unusual gift with words. You have both a good vocabulary and a way with words. Develop this trait even more. The ability to express yourself adequately will separate you from the average person and give you a sense of confidence.

Learn to choose your words wisely. Once said, the impact is felt. Never clutter your mind or mouth with foul words. They will harm, not build. Learn words of expression and tenderness.

Library

I was impressed with how you used the library at Southern Methodist University tonight. While I was talking to the library researcher, you moved directly to the cross-index file and found what you needed on the golden section. Our study of this unique geometric concept was exciting. We found that the golden section not only relates to geometry, but also to music, art, architecture, and almost any element of proportion.

Several weeks ago you also used the library effectively to do a research project on great mathematicians. This effort reminds us of the vast material available in libraries. We know so little, don't we? So much information is available! I made it through the University of Florida, because I learned to use the library resources. You are doing the same while still in junior high school. Expand this knowledge. Sometimes go to the library and just roam to see all that's available.

A library is a good example of stored data. It's not really helpful until used. The same can be true of our own stored data. We can learn to apply it in our lives.

Ability

In our uniqueness it becomes obvious that each of us has different abilities. I was pleasantly surprised several days ago by the teaching ability of one of our employees. Because it's natural to excel in certain things and to be less knowledgeable in others, we ought to strive to determine those areas of natural ability.

You have a natural ability in relation to numbers and in analytical matters. You need to recognize this and use it for the maximum good. This ability can carry over from numbers to logical thought patterns. This reasoning process will be very important in achieving business success.

While some ability seems to be natural, we can train ourselves to be effective in areas in which we don't have that natural feel. This expands our horizons beautifully. God's Word teaches that from those to whom much is given, much is required. You are one of those to whom God has given much ability. Learn to use all of it and to develop new abilities. It's frustrating not to be able to use one's ability, and very rewarding to test our abilities to the limit.

Writing

This past year I have tried to write you a note each day. It has been fun to write down my thoughts on different subjects. It requires a mental discipline that is good. For our current session on Galatians in my Sunday-school class, I am also writing my lesson notes and having them typed and sent to all my class members. I've found that writing overcomes my tendency to be too casual in my approach.

While I believe this kind of writing is effective, I dislike having to write memos. They are too formal. I like the personal contact better. Some write memos as a defense mechanism. I find this to be a weak tool in business. Of course, at times things do need to be written to be documented.

Both you and Val are good writers. I love to read your various reports. They are informative and to the point without a lot of fluff. Yesterday, Arthur Blessitt called and said his new book, a novel, is off the presses. Arthur touches people because he can relate to them where they are. I believe both you and Val have a similar ability. Use it to accomplish the most possible.

Home

You are a part of a God-ordained institution—the home. While God formed and gave direction to the home, God is not in control of each home.

The happy home is one in which God is in complete control and each member of the home is following God's instructions. The Bible teaches us our individual responsibility within the home. When these instructions are followed, the home is complete and beautiful.

The home is intended to be a haven—a safe place to relax, to strengthen ourselves for the tasks of life.

See the home for what it is to be. Don't take it for granted. Help build the home to what it can become. Look forward to the day when you'll be building a home in which God has ordained you to be the spiritual leader.

Heir

In the last several months we've been learning a lot about the heirs to the estate of Howard Hughes. The fight for the two billion dollars is on and will be a long, drawn-out affair. I've never been an heir in anyone's will; yet as a Christian, I can understand the benefits of being an heir. Christ established a will—in fact, a perfect will—and I'm a beneficiary.

You, Val, and Mom are heirs to my estate, if I have anything when I die. Yet, I hope that you are heir to more than mere financial resources.

What you are is largely the results of your family life—what's being provided for you. God gave you your natural characteristics and abilities, and our home life has helped shape them. Where the shaping was good, be thankful; where the effort caused any misshaping, forgive us and ask God to reshape you perfectly.

You are an heir of God—a joint heir with Christ. You are an heir of your mom and me. You are an heir to your culture and your country. Use these rights and benefits as an heir to strengthen and direct your life.

Adrenaline

At times we find we have extra reserves of strength or a strong sense of enthusiasm to get a job done. Many times this is caused by a natural body function where our needs trigger our adrenal glands to pump adrenaline into our systems.

The need can be physical, such as the time I got my army jeep hung up on a big boulder and needed extra strength to lift it off. It can also be psychological, such as when we get into tight spots and our minds race to find the solutions.

Today, the adrenaline has been pumping great. First, I've had a busier schedule than usual—some items being real irritants. Yet, I've had an inner strength to face these problems and get them solved.

God created us with this inner reserve. We need to recognize that it will be there when we need it. This physical reserve, along with the inner strength that comes from our spiritual lives, combines to give us vast potential to solve crises when they come.

Rest

As much rest as you get, you might feel there's no need to consider this particular subject. But it's important—even God ordained.

God created us with a need for a certain amount of rest. This balance gives our bodies and minds a necessary break from everyday physical and mental pressures. Many types of sickness can often be avoided simply by getting an adequate amount of rest.

Rest and recreation are needed in our lives to refresh us for the main tasks of life. It's not isolated from our other function, but is, rather, an integral part. We need to learn to get enough rest to be prepared for our other key activities.

Rest can come in many ways—reading, studying, even physical work. The key is doing something different from our regular responsibilities.

Rest! It's good. But don't let it rule your entire life. Measure it and discipline yourself not to overdo it. Be well balanced.

Energy

Energy is a key word in our world today. Man is using his sources of energy faster than he can produce them. He is depleting some of these sources. But man has never fully tapped the source of personal energy.

Let's consider your source of energy. Obviously your physical well-being is important. Your food intake, diet, rest, exercise, and physical development affect the amount of energy available to you. All of us know this. But there are additional resources upon which to draw. One is the mental process. It has been estimated that more than one-half of all illness is mental in nature. We can mentally train ourselves to fully utilize our efforts. Your body will create energy.

Our spiritual health also produces or becomes a drain on energy. Peace with God and reconciliation between God and man, and man with man, brings us to a point where we have our energy levels at the highest point. So take care of your physical, mental, and spiritual life to create the energy you need for a wonderful life.

Resources

Life is a series of activities in which we utilize resources to accomplish what we set out to do. All around us we have resources at hand that can make our lives fuller and happier.

The company I work for has what it calls "replenishable resources." The forest can be cut, then replanted, and used again in fifty years. Many of our resources are like that. In fact, the resource of friendship builds so that it becomes more and more useful to us.

You can see and find resources for life all around you. Look for them! Learn to tap them! Your ability to use these resources to a large degree will determine your success in life. This is true for all areas—financial, family, social, and spiritual.

You not only should learn to use life's resources, but even to be a resource for others. To be resourceful in helping others brings tremendous personal joy.

Power

I overheard you and Valerie discussing the concept of power recently. It's very important that you seek God's leadership in determining the proper definition and use of power.

In the first place, we should never seek after power. It's not a worthy goal in itself. It's true that in an orderly society some people have a degree of control over others, but that control must be meted out fairly and for the good of all concerned.

After all, what is power?

Some foolishly say money is power!
Others fall into the trap of thinking intellectualism is
    power!
Still others think the control of people and their futures
    and fortunes is power!

Real power is none of these! The most powerful man who ever lived and who affected our world more than any other was Jesus Christ. He did not seek financial gain nor were His teachings only theoretical, nor did He desire the role of earthly lord! Rather, His power came from His giving nature. His whole purpose was to come so that we could have an abundant life. Real power, then, even for us, comes from God Himself.

Peace

Today is a good day to thank God for the relative peace we have in the world. On December 7, 1941, began what came to be known as World War II. The bombing of Pearl Harbor forced America to declare war on Japan the next day. Later, in 1942, we declared war on Germany.

Peace is a fragile thing. We must guard it jealously. This is true both on an international and national basis, and also on a personal basis.

International peace can be protected by working hard with our world neighbors.

Personal peace can be attained by harmonizing the various forces within our lives.

National peace will come when God is given preeminence in our nation.

Personal peace will come when God controls our lives.

Because peace is so fragile, we need to learn how we can have it. Personal peace comes only through God's perfect direction in our lives. God's Word tells us we can have it; so we should claim this precious promise. It's promised to those who are controlled by God and empowered by His Holy Spirit. The peace of God and peace with God are ours if we follow His will.

Saving

What people save tells a lot about them. I love to clean out houses and discard unneeded things. Some people never learn what or how to save. If you develop that trait (which you already have) it can lead to a happier life.

Obviously it's important to save money, so you can pay for what you'll need or want later. This kind of saving is good, but it should never become the controlling goal in life.

But I think you should learn to save other things: ideas! fun times! letters! precious moments! These things will bring you tremendous joy later in life.

Saving is the opposite of waste. Don't waste your money, your time, your effort. Don't waste your years with your family. Make the most of them. What you save from these experiences will go a long way to make your future happier.

Profit

Today is the last day of the first quarter of this year. My company made its first quarterly profit in several years. It's exciting to see the turnabout—to be a part of a winning team.

Profit is an essential aspect of the business formula. In home building if we properly mix property, product, policies, procedures, planning, and people, we are almost guaranteed a profit. We've done that this year. There's no question, either, that people are the most important ingredient. People make profit. The best product in the world won't guarantee profit.

Profits enable us to grow, to expand. We can meet more housing needs, and employ more people. We can also eventually return to our shareholders' capital; so it can be reinvested. The economic cycle is beautiful when it's in balance. Profits help keep it in balance. Without profits, the economy dries up, unemployment goes up, and government has to step up its welfare programs. The answer is a healthy, profitable economy.

Interest

The kind of interest I want to share with you today is economic interest on investments. You and I had our savings passbook posted today, and they credited to our account many dollars in interest. Boy, that felt good! For the right to use our savings, they paid us a good price.

Today we took some of our resources out of savings, where we were getting guaranteed earnings, to invest in stocks where any gain is speculative. Before we earn anything, we have to assess for ourselves the cost of funds invested—the interest we would have earned in savings.

Interest rates fluctuate almost daily. They seem to affect our economy more than almost any other single factor. Our success as home builders this year depends on the interest rates we can get for our customers.

The use of money should always have assigned to it an economic value. So, as you think about investments, be sure to consider the cost of money—interest.

Rent

A basic factor in economics is the concept of rent. In lay terms it's defined as the amount paid or received for the use of the capital of others. We can pay rent for the use of land, physical improvements, equipment, or even money. In the case of money, rent is equivalent to interest.

This past week at work we tested the economics of purchasing a radio unit as compared to renting it. We found when taking everything into consideration it would pay to purchase rather than rent.

In our business we encourage home ownership rather than renting. It has several advantages: deductibility of interest for tax purposes, buildup of equity in the home, and pride of ownership. The key advantage to renting is mobility. Leases are usually short term. Renting doesn't commit a person for a long period of time.

On a national basis, renting is big business: cars, equipment, office space. Anything man needs he can usually rent. Understanding the concept of rent will be important as you get older and face economic decisions.

Numbers

Numbers can be used for evil or good. I've seen how people can take numbers and supposedly "prove" all kinds of things with them. I was in a meeting with a man who started telling us what all the numbers meant: one, unity; two, union; and so on. Of course, on this basis we can come up with all kinds of meanings, even though forced a little.

There is a sense of order with numbers. As a CPA I can sense that order and like the feel. As a young man, I'd encourage you to learn all you can about numbers—their various functions and relationships. Go as high in mathematics and related subjects as you can. You will be competing in a number-oriented society.

I've seen where I could sell a project with numbers where it would be impossible to sell the same idea with only words. Numbers are believable. There's a fixed quality about them on which we can rely. A good feel for numbers will aid in your basic logic. It helps sort things out in a sequential manner. The way learning is increasing, you'll need as much number training as possible.

Wealth

What is wealth? My college economics book had a chapter called "Weal and Wealth." I found out that I didn't know the real meaning of either word. Wealth obviously has economic connotations. But how do you measure it? As a child I had wealth in relation to some people; yet my family had hardly enough on which to live. So economic wealth is relative.

But wealth is more than money or things. We hear it said, "He has a wealth of data stored away." This wealth of data can possibly be converted into economic gain. On the other hand, it can be totally wasted. Wealth isn't real until converted.

I believe real wealth centers on mental and spiritual resources. This is what brings joy. Today I was visiting with a very wealthy man, economically, who shared that he felt empty, without any resources, until just several weeks ago when he turned his life totally over to God. Fantastic! Wealth comes not by receiving but giving! By first giving of himself to God, he received God's ultimate blessing: love, joy, peace. He now feels like a wealthy man for the first time in his life.

Poverty

We are as rich as we think we are, and we're as poor as we think we are. Until we had the means of instant communication through the use of radio and television, people could not easily compare their positions in relation to others. They were more content because of the lack of comparison.

Poverty is hard to meaningfully define. The federal government has adopted an "economic poverty level"; yet many people within this economic level don't consider themselves living in poverty. On the other hand, many who make more money consider themselves very poor.

Looking back at my youth, we had to be considered fairly poor; yet I never knew it. I never was aware of not having everything I needed or wanted. I saw others with a lot less.

We need to relate to those who have little of life's material blessings with love and help. While happiness doesn't depend on having plenty, it's important to have necessities. It's hard to reach a man for Christ when he's hungry, so if we want to evangelize, it's important to relate to the total man and his total needs.

Endowed

We are endowed by our Creator! Yes, God did endow you with what you are. God also uses other means to endow you. He used your mother and me. A lot of us is in you. You are a composite of a lot of influences in your life.

The endowment becomes the now material. How it's developed is up to you. A person can completely waste a monetary endowment, and he can also waste his other endowments. You have a spiritual endowment that came down from people like Grandmama Susie, all of your grandparents, and your mom and dad. But, ultimately, what you do to mature spiritually is up to *you*.

You are also endowed with good looks. Be thankful—not conceited. Conceit in a man is really objectionable. Your endowment also runs to your mental capabilities. Sharpen them to a point of usefulness to your fellow man.

Plan well so you can leave your own endowment for the future. Be thankful for what has been endowed you by God: your family, your country, and all mankind. Recognize it and use it effectively.

Giving

All my life and all your life, we've heard our pastor, Sunday-school teachers, and friends talk about the tithe or the tithing of our resources. It's very important not to think of the tithe as an end in itself, as merely something to do. It's of little importance, unless it's done with the right spirit and motive.

I believe in tithing—the giving on a consistent basis a portion of my income to my church. I see it as the only practical means for my church to plan and grow. But, remember, that's only a small part of the biblical part of stewardship. Romans 6:13 says, ". . . give yourself completely to God—every part of you . . ." (LB). It becomes obvious that I haven't met God's command when I've given the 10 percent outlined in the Old Testament.

We began increasing our 10 percent fourteen years ago. We now double tithe to our church on a regular basis and have given over one-third of our total income for a number of years. Yet, God wants *me*. He doesn't need my money. So. I'm only accomplishing His purpose when I give Him everything: my money, my time, my abilities, my family, my social and civic relationships. Only then am I following His instructions. Giving this way is great fun!

Gifts

Today I got around to doing some shopping. There's nothing I would rather do than give gifts, but there's only one drawback; there's also nothing that I like to do less than shopping. Five days before Christmas is early for me. I'm thankful for Mom and her willingness to get the shopping done.

There's very little that I really want or need; so I like those specially thought-out gifts that are very personal, like the one you have for Mom. She will have that for a lifetime and will always remember her wonderful son who made it especially for her.

I've always enjoyed getting gifts for you, especially clothes. For one thing, you wear clothes well and look good in them. And you've always seemed to enjoy your gifts. You need to be careful not to take gift giving for granted or to fail to thank those who give you gifts.

At this time of year we need to be reminded of the best gift in all of life—Jesus Christ. And also your best gift—yourself. Give of yourself freely and openly, and lovingly. You are a wonderful gift.

Thanksgiving

Today, as we think about all that we've got for which to be thankful, we should realize how good God has been to us. As a family, all of us have good health; we have active, aggressive minds that we're willing to use to learn and grow.

We also have all we need from a material standpoint. Not that we have used our financial resources for excessive personal pleasures; yet all our basic needs have been met. As we give thanks for this, we also need to review our basic stewardship of all we have.

I regularly thank God for your growth. While you need to

grow socially, you have grown mentally, and you seem to be tapping your mental capabilities. Now you need to broaden your personal goals, to be more explosive as your life branches out in many new exciting directions.

God has been very good to us. Let's be sure to give Him thanks continually.

Contributions

We're called on regularly to contribute to some special effort. Usually our contributions are of a monetary nature, but sometimes we're called on to give ourselves more directly. Today a Christian brother said to me, "Fred, I need *you*." He's not after dollars specifically but advice and help in shaping a direction for the future.

In the last ten years I've given away a good portion of my income. But I don't regret one penny I've ever given to help someone less fortunate or to help someone find the joys of the Christian life.

Learn early to maximize your personal contributions to as many causes as possible. You'll be the beneficiary.

Surprise

One of the most exciting things in life is to receive a surprise. I love to surprise others, especially Mom, Val, and you. I also like surprises. The best gifts I've ever received are those that were real surprises like the special book Mom put together after my ten years at General Development Corporation.

Sometimes we don't think to add that special zest to life. At the office I find employees more appreciative of two hours off on a special day, when it's a surprise, than getting the entire day off when they're expecting it.

There are some surprises to avoid—those that are negative in nature. Don't wait to the end of a grading period to tell us of a low grade. In that case, preparation is better than surprise. Also, never surprise someone who is depending on you. If you can't help them, let them know ahead of time.

I always love to surprise Mom at bonus time. I'll never forget both of our being thrilled because of the surprise of that first bonus check. The most joy we have now in the surprises of life relate to you and Val. You are a great surprise!

Spice

Man attempts to add spice to his life through a myriad of ways. "The spice of life"—it's something different for each of us, and it changes from time to time in an individual's life. My point today is that there are all kinds of things that will add that extra little spice to your life.

Spice is used to flavor—to make food more palatable or delicious. Just as spices vary in different parts of our country and around the world, so, too, do the things that add that extra zing to a person's life.

Some spices are good for us, and some are not so good. Even too much of your much-loved A-1 sauce wouldn't be too good for you. You should find those things in life that add to life and at the same time have no bad side effects.

I see some of the spices of life to be: a special friend, a private retreat, a good restaurant, an exciting book, a sense of accomplishment, a good deed, a hard job, a wink from someone special. All these and many more can add to your joy of life. You, too, can add spice to the lives of others.

Blessings

I love the song "Count Your Blessings." As I count my blessings, it reminds me how good God has been to me.

God Himself is life's greatest blessing!
My family is a very special blessing from God.

I thank God regularly for the blessing provided me in my
   work.
Our church is a fantastic blessing.
America the Beautiful is a real blessing!

I can go on and on and thank God for so many blessings. This
is a good exercise. It disciplines us to recognize all the good
things in our lives.

Not everything in life will happen just the way we want. Yet we
have so much more than many people. We have all we need
materially. We have spiritual blessings to celebrate. Life has
brought us a diversity that few enjoy.

Because of our blessings, we have an equal responsibility.
God's Word says, "Much is required from those to whom much
is given, for their responsibility is greater" (*see* Luke 12:48).

You have been given much—physically, intellectually, socially,
and spiritually. Share these beautiful blessings of life with
others.

Spiritual Gifts

This past weekend we talked about the church and how God
gave the church—the people of God—spiritual gifts to accomplish the ultimate purpose of the church. We showed where
God's Word tells us that all of us are given a spiritual gift—or
many gifts in some cases—and that as we use these gifts within
the church, we are accomplishing God's purpose.

I believe one of your spiritual gifts is being a leader. Recognize
that this gift comes from God and that you are responsible to
Him for the stewardship of this gift. You are planning to utilize
this gift as a camp counselor, and you're even planning for leadership roles in other areas of church life, which is great.

Also, use this gift in all aspects of your life—at home, at school,
and in the community. God gives it to you for that purpose; so
that you can be a Christian witness.

Help others sense their spiritual gifts. Thank them for using
their gifts such as preaching, teaching, giving, sharing, helping,
and encouraging. All these and more are gifts to us from God.

Beauty

Life is beautiful! Our environment is beautiful! People are beautiful! There is around us enough beauty for us to fill our cups continually:

in the brightness of a new, fresh day;
in the activity of a hectic day of work;
in the relationships of life;
in the dusk of day as the sun sets;
in the excitement of the night;
in the peace that comes at sleep.

See beauty everywhere. Learn to look for it in everything. As you live, help create beauty. God made the ultimate beauty, and He gave man a responsibility to care both for His creation and to take the initiative to create beauty in his own life and around him. Be sensitive to this responsibility.

Learning to enjoy beauty will help you enjoy life. See it in people, children's faces, beautiful girls, the lines of age in an oldster's smile. Learn also to see beauty in how God cares for every need, in every situation. It's great! Beautiful!

Joy

Today I had the opportunity to speak at the morning worship service at the First Baptist Church of South Miami. I chose the subject "The Joy of the Journey." Tonight Arthur Blessitt preached, and his message centered on our need to rejoice in all that God has done for us.

We need to consider all the reasons for joy in our lives. It's easy for me, because God has been so good to me: a wonderful wife, two great kids of whom I'm so proud, a good company to work for with fine fellow employees, a church to worship and serve where God is honored, good health, good friends, and on and on the list goes.

The ultimate blessing, though, is the beauty of Jesus Christ within me and you. Sensing this causes the greatest joy. The joy He brings us flows into and from our lives like an artesian well—never ending.

Joy is a positive feeling. We should strive to cultivate this positiveness in our lives, to never let the pressing in of the world rob us of the tremendous joy that is ours.

Singing

I love to sing! Tonight at the First Baptist Church in Rockwall, Texas, I was asked to lead the singing as we shared together, "This I Affirm, God's Love Gift to You."

Later someone came up to me and *affirmed* this in me—that I don't have the gift of singing. While I don't have the gift, I still have the joy.

When I'm down and need a lift, I've found all I need is to lift a prayer to God and to sing praises to Christ. My heart is immediately renewed!

I'm really thankful for your being in the two church choirs. Your participation in the choir helps you, and it helps others in their worship experience. You're young enough to learn "how" to sing, to make the most of your God-given ability.

Last week I saw the possibilities of what music can do as I was brought close to God as the soloist sang "The Holy City." Music is worship! Music is also an aid to worship. It is used effectively to prepare us for an encounter with God.

Music has always meant a lot to me. While on those military-police posts in Germany, I sang over and over again the beautiful hymns and choruses that I learned as a youngster. It was a way I could draw close to God and He to me.

Happiness

Happiness is Bobby after a week of camp, getting special treatment for his chigger bites. Happiness is seeing Valerie walking to the stage to receive her high-school diploma with honors. Happiness is seeing Mom share her excitement in Christ at a lay-renewal weekend.

Happiness is those very special times that we will remember forever. Happiness is also those little things that we'll soon forget; yet they bring us tremendous "joy on the journey."

Happiness is determined by frame of mind, not by circumstances. Happiness comes through acceptance—acceptance of ourselves, others, and acceptance of our current situations. Happiness is a mental process. I can tell myself, generally, to be happy and I will be happy. Happiness is also related in my spiritual life. When I'm satisfied that I'm in God's will, it's much easier to be happy.

I'm thankful for your happy nature. It's infectious and moves to others easily, especially within your family. Happiness is to know my Saviour and to have a son like you.

Smile

My favorite sticker of Arthur Blessitt's reads SMILE, GOD LOVES YOU. We ought to smile more. It's contagious. It makes others feel better when we're smiling.

You have a great smile. Use it more. You are the most handsome when you're smiling. A smile is a bridge of friendship with family, friends, and others with whom you come into contact.

A smile breaks down barriers, so that you will have an easier time relating to other people. It makes others feel comfortable with you. It generates trust. It can be the first step in a meaningful relationship.

Let smiling become natural, so everyone can enjoy it. Try it more with your mother, dad, and sister. We love you and that great smile of yours.

Treasure

The Bible teaches: "For where your treasure is, there will your heart be also" (Matthew 6:21). We tend to go in the direction of the priorities we set for ourselves. If we seek financial gain, we set priorities that help us meet that goal. Whatever we tend to treasure in life, we work at and commit ourselves to.

I wanted you and me to use that expensive "treasure finder" to discover real relics and valuable treasures. All we ever found were nickels, dimes, bottle tops, and aluminum foil. But there's a lesson to be learned from that. Our finder was only as good as its operators—you and me. And we never took it seriously enough.

So, if we are to find the real treasures of life, we must train ourselves to find them. There are a lot of things to sidetrack us—like the aluminum foil—but we must stick to it and develop successful techniques.

Don't be fooled by gaudy treasures. Seek the real thing. Intangible treasures are more often than not much better than mere tangibles that will ultimately be worth nothing.

Solitude

This weekend as Mom and I went off to the Church Council Retreat and as Valerie went to visit the Baylor University campus, you were left at home overnight alone for the first time. For us it wasn't a hard decision to make because of your independence and maturity.

As you grow older, you'll be alone more often—away on trips, away at college, Even though you were alone in one respect, you had someone with you—on TV, in the books you were reading, and, of course, you have Christ's constant companionship.

Since we live in a fast-moving society, we need to be alone at times for solace and personal meditation. It's a time when we can reorient our lives and set goals. It can be a refreshing, life-building time.

Use the time when you're alone well. Don't waste it. Be creative and motivate yourself to a more effective life. Then those times alone will be worth while and never dreaded.

Free

I like to be free. It's comfortable to be loose, relaxed—not tied down. This sense of freedom comes more from our attitudes than the circumstances of life.

I can be involved in a number of different activities and still be free. God's Word says: "You will know the truth, and the truth will make you free" (John 8:32 RSV).

This kind of freedom makes us free:

from anxiety and tension!

from social pressure!

from sin and its results!

from lack of direction!

from self-guilt!

It's a beautiful freedom, but it was paid for with a price—the death of Jesus Christ—for you and for me. You also enjoy certain freedoms provided you as a member of your family, and you enjoy freedoms within our country, because others paid the price of freedom.

Yes, you can be free because of what others did for you; so claim it, enjoy it, and learn how to set others free.

Books

During your lifetime you will probably read several thousand books. Learn to choose wisely in the selection of books. They will have an impact on you, so be careful. Not that you should fear books in which the author has a point of view different from your own, but be critical in your personal evaluation. Don't let the author sneak up on you.

Read books of all kinds. Let them broaden you but not influence you to the point where you stand for nothing. Learn to evaluate the authors and background from which they are writing. Some books attempt a fairness in approach; others are pure propaganda. Learn to spot bias and bigotry.

Use books as learning tools for facts, history, human nature, religion, and all kinds of information. Learn not to waste time with useless books or books that lead to a narrow approach to life. Books that people give you tell you something about them. This is helpful in evaluating the desirability of reading a particular book.

Bible

The most important book ever written is the Bible. It is also the hardest for some people to understand. Since the Bible really is God's Word, we need to seek God's leadership when we're reading it. That's why I always pray for God's Holy Spirit to direct me as I study God's Word.

Accept the fact that we will not understand everything about the Bible. But don't use that as a reason not to seek God's direction from His Word. Never argue about the Bible or try to prove it. It speaks for itself. Accept it in faith.

I love the precious promises from the Bible. They strengthen me as I face the tasks of life.

God can change man, and God's Word can lead men to God. Therefore, if we want others to know God, we need to share His Good News with them. As you draw on its resources, it will strengthen your life.

Government

Government is so big it baffles most of us. Yet, it's important that as private citizens we learn all we can, so we can help shape government and its vast bureaucracy.

Who, or what, is the government? Some would say it's the bureaucracy that we've talked about before. Others would naively say it's the people. Some would be satisfied to identify it as our political system. None of these are completely adequate.

In lay terms we can say it involves all these. It's the means by which we, the governed, decide to best meet our common needs. These needs relate to our economic needs, our social needs, our needs for defense, education, and on and on the list goes.

We have a good form of government. Yet, we know it's far from perfect. So, some use their combined influence to make changes. Always be sure that your voice is heard. Don't lose any of your present rights by default. Always consider the good of the majority of the governed. Here, again, we see the need to be unselfish as we view government and its role.

Income Tax

Today our federal income-tax returns are due. I believe mine was mailed yesterday. I always have a sense of pride as I pay my taxes. I get pleasure out of helping finance our government. Not that I agree with all they do; yet men and women selected by all Americans make the decisions.

I've never knowingly claimed anything on my tax return that was not proper. If I've had any question, I've always favored the government.

With tax reforms in the last several years there is more equity in the tax laws; yet more reforms need to be made. Special-interest groups have lobbied hard to protect their tax breaks. All of them aren't bad. It's a way of economically justifying a particular industry that could not exist within the regular tax structure.

Pay every penny of tax you owe, thankful for the right, and try as a citizen to see that it's well spent by exercising your right as a voter.

Veterans

Today is Veterans Day. It used to be called Armistice Day, because it is the day World War I ended with the signing of the armistice. It is also the birthday of your granddad—Mom's father—who was a veteran.

America owes a lot to its veterans, especially those who were injured while serving their country. As a veteran myself, I'm thankful for the GI Bill that helped provide my education and also for my veterans' insurance program.

We should honor our veterans and at the same time work toward their complete reentry into the American life-style. This should not amount to doing for them more than we would for others who also serve their country. It's a matter of national respect, not national welfare.

Hopefully, we can look back at the cost of past wars and avoid such world conflicts in the future. Now we can be thankful for peace and those who helped provide for it.

America

Today I've been considering the greatness of America and the causes for that greatness. Tomorrow I'll be speaking at Arthur Blessitt's state-wide rally in Concord, New Hampshire. As I consider what I'll share, my mind comes to that song, "I'm Thankful to Be an American." This song expresses the deep personal feelings of my heart. I'm praying that God will work through me to verbalize properly this beautiful truth.

America *is* a great nation! It has great resources, and it has used these resources to share with a needy world. These resources are tangible—the key being our excess food supplies and our great industrial base. But the resources that we've shared include intangibles—our concept of freedom and the rights of man and our Christian belief whereby *all men* can be reconciled to God through Jesus Christ.

America is also great in its vitality! We are a resilient people. We have faced hardships and have come through a stronger and more united people. America is great in its opportunity! Fresh horizons are open to us. Our task is to be up to it—to match our personal potential to the great potential of our beautiful America.

Index